A TEACHE
STUDENT

MW01146387

TEACHING, ENGAGING, AND THRIVING IN HIGHER ED

James M. Lang and Michelle D. Miller, SERIES EDITORS

A TEACHER'S GUIDE TO LEARNING STUDENT NAMES

Why You Should, Why It's Hard, How You Can

MICHELLE D. MILLER

University of Oklahoma Press : Norman

Library of Congress Cataloging-in-Publication Data

Names: Miller, Michelle D., 1968– author.
Title: A teacher's guide to learning student names : why you
    should, why it's hard, how you can / Michelle D. Miller.
Description: Norman : University of Oklahoma Press, 2024. |
    Series: Teaching, engaging, and thriving in higher education;
    vol 2 | Summary: "An accessible how-to guide for teachers
    in higher education who struggle to learn their students'
    names"—Provided by publisher.
Identifiers: LCCN 2024014092 | ISBN 978-0-8061-9466-0
    (paperback)
Subjects: LCSH: Teacher-student relationships. | Educational
    psychology. | Motivation in education. | Recollection
    (Psychology) | BISAC: EDUCATION / Teaching / Methods &
    Strategies | EDUCATION / Classroom Management
Classification: LCC LB1033 .M543 2024 |
    DDC 371.102/3—dc23/eng/20240511
LC record available at https://lccn.loc.gov/2024014092

*A Teacher's Guide to Learning Student Names: Why You Should, Why
It's Hard, How You Can* is Volume 2 in the Teaching, Engaging,
and Thriving in Higher Ed series.

The paper in this book meets the guidelines for permanence and
durability of the Committee on Production Guidelines for Book
Longevity of the Council on Library Resources, Inc. ∞

For my students, especially the ones whose names I forgot.

CONTENTS

INTRODUCTION

One of my first and hardest lessons as a beginning college teacher was on the subject of learning students' names. My first semester of teaching consisted of running my own breakout sessions—which, at the enormous state university where I did my graduate work, were essentially mini-classes assigned to individual teaching assistants (TAs). By way of preparation, I had put together lots of carefully crafted slides for the overhead projector, outlined and scripted formal lectures capturing in detail the findings and controversies of the day. In class, I had stood confidently and projected my voice all the way to the back row, spicing things up with just the right sprinkling of pop culture references and passing around stacks of the detailed handouts I'd labored over the night before.

By my own estimation, I had nailed it. Then the student evaluations came in.

There were all the usual critiques that are typical of rookie college teachers: too much emphasis on my own presentation, not enough interaction, reams of facts without context on why anyone should care. But the real gut punch was this, a single short comment that simply read, *"She didn't even try to learn our names."*

They were right. Not only had I not succeeded, but I hadn't really tried. In all the preparation I did—indeed reflecting a focus on my own performance, rather than on students' engagement—learning names fell completely off my list of priorities.

In the wake of that first bruising round of feedback, I set to work at getting better at teaching. After I landed a faculty job at a teaching-focused institution, I focused on mastering the basics of responsive, student-focused pedagogy. Eventually, I improved enough to be honored with an institution-wide teaching award. This helped inspire me to begin writing for other faculty members about techniques that tap into learning science and that also help create a classroom atmosphere that's welcoming to all students.

As part of that journey of professional growth, I realized I'd need to come back to the tough issue of learning names. I continued to struggle with that one, and still do today, for reasons that will become clear through the course of this short book.

Like many instructors, I approached that aspiration to get better at name learning with a mix of unrealistic optimism, a nagging sense of dread, and a misty magical-thinking vision in which *this* semester would be different. I kept expecting it to be easier than it was, suspecting that all the other teachers—the ones calling out personal greetings to students they ran into, calling on folks during the vibrant classes I could see through open classroom doors on my trips up and down the halls—somehow had it easier. Surely for *them*, it all happened naturally and without the struggle I was going through each and every semester.

I really should have known better. This is because I'd spent the whole first part of my academic career in the research field of psycholinguistics, concentrating specifically on the intersection between memory and language processing. As cognitive psychologists in training, my lab mates and I had been working to untangle exactly how the mind takes in and saves information at the mind-blowing speed of spoken conversation, and how our ability to do this changes as a function of various factors including prior knowledge, the grammatical structures being used, and aging.[1]

At the time, our field had been rocked by a new set of research findings that drove home the difference between learning proper names and learning other kinds of words. I explore these concepts more in the next chapter, but in short, what researchers discovered was this: words that happen to be a person's name are incredibly hard to turn into lasting memories, and harder still to pull out of memory once they are in there.[2] When researchers totaled up all the mental processes that have to happen in order to form lasting associations between a more-or-less arbitrary set of sounds and one specific person in the world, it started to look like a miracle that we *ever* manage to learn a name, and completely unsurprising that we usually fail.

Now, much older and (somewhat) wiser, I'm putting the ideas into practice. As sociologist Kurt Lewin famously said, nothing is as practical as a good theory, and theories of verbal memory turn out to explain not only why names are difficult to learn but also why certain techniques work, and they spark ideas for creating new techniques. Putting theory into practice may not have made me the world's champion at name learning, but it's made me worlds better than I was before.

That's what I wrote this short handbook to do—to share with you the most critical concepts about name learning that all teachers should know, to dispel myths and misconceptions about remembering names, and to teach you the techniques that are the most likely to work. No matter where you are in your quest to get better at this aspect of teaching—whether it's just to have a solid percentage of them down by end of the semester or to pull off the feat of learning a whole class of thirty plus perfectly on the first day—there will be techniques that will move you closer to your goal.

Besides being a cognitive psychologist, I bring a few other things to the table that will, I think, give this book a special niche in this often-discussed aspect of teaching skill. I've long been an enthusiast for talking to fellow faculty about teaching, especially about how ideas drawn from cognitive psychology and brain science can make teaching more rewarding for us and more effective for our students.[3]

To be clear, though, none of these qualities or experiences make me a natural whiz at learning names. The opposite is very much true, due to another challenge piled on top of the difficulties inherent to the task (which you'll be well acquainted with a few pages from now). I have a mild variation of a perceptual and cognitive problem known formally as *prosopagnosia* and casually as face blindness. When I finally figured this out well into adulthood, it explained a lot about why recognizing people visually never seemed to work the same way for me as it did for other people.

Like other people with this same problem, I *see* faces just fine. The difficulty comes later when I try to connect facial features to a person's identity. Especially when I meet similar-appearing people in the same context (twentysomething women with brown hair in a class, middle-aged men with facial hair at a conference), I have considerable trouble telling faces apart. This difficulty forces me to rely more heavily on other cues, such as voices, hairstyle, or clothing. That old idea that "I can't remember names, but never forget a face" must be reversed in my case, or I'd barely be able to tell who is who in my daily life. We'll discuss more strategies for coping with face-recognition difficulties later in the book. But for now, suffice it to say that I've had to be very planful about this part of my teaching practice, which gives me both empathy for and a special ability to give advice to those who struggle with names for any and all kinds of reasons.

Regardless of whether you find learning names really hard or not too bad, now is a particularly good time to hone this aspect of teaching skill. Most people have heard the old saw from Dale Carnegie (of *How to Win Friends and Influence People* fame) that "a person's name is to that person the sweetest and most important sound in any language." For college teachers, however, the importance of names goes well beyond the salesy social skills that Carnegie was pushing. As professors Kelly Hogan and Viji Sathy emphasize in their influential book *Inclusive Teaching: Structures for Promoting Equity in the College Classroom*,[4] learning names—and saying them correctly!—is a major aspect of inclusive, equity-oriented teaching, one that supports success for more diverse learners. This theme echoes throughout other advice on creating inclusive classrooms.[5] For teachers committed to fighting bias and systemic exclusion—which, today, ought to be all of us—name learning is a critical skill. It might even have beneficial psychological effects, according to the authors of the book *Improving Learning and Mental Health in the College Classroom.*[6]

Research also backs up the idea that hearing their names used makes students feel more engaged and supported by their instructors. One study (discussed later in more depth) polled students in a large science course on their perceptions of name usage in class. The authors concluded from the data that "the majority of students (85 percent) felt as though instructors knowing their names was important. Students described that when instructors know their names, they feel more valued in the course and frequently mentioned that they feel as though they are more than just a face in a crowd."[7]

Names also tie into a core question about higher education revealed by the COVID-19 pandemic: what is the value of face-to-face, in-person instruction, and what, if anything, is lost when interaction moves online? It stands to reason that if we and our students are going to deal with the risk and put in the effort to have face-to-face class meetings, we should make the most of that time together. Learning names is one small part of this enormous issue, but if doing it enhances this costly in-person experience in any way, it should be a priority.

It is true that the face-to-face modality is where actually remembering names is the most relevant. In fully online modalities, names are usually right there and available either in the discussion posts and messages we exchange in asynchronous classes, or superimposed on the voices and faces we see within the video-conferences that are common in synchronous classes. That said, the concepts in this book are still valuable for instructors teaching mostly or entirely online. Toward the end of the book, there are suggestions on correct pronunciation, which is important when recording audio feedback or interacting online in real time. Considering the techniques and rationale for effectively using student names will also help us stay focused on the importance of personalizing our interactions with students as we communicate within online courses. Finally, basic name-learning techniques are valuable in a variety of professional contexts—disciplinary conferences, administrative meetings, and other settings where communicative and interpersonal skills are key. In sum, while in-person settings are the main ones I had in mind when writing this book, the skills discussed within it and the values it promotes are for everyone.

These techniques are also going to be especially useful for a large and still-growing segment of professional educators: adjunct instructors in higher education, who often cover a large and frequently changing set of courses, sometimes at multiple institutions spread around a given geographic area. There are many well-documented challenges and inequities associated with holding adjunct status; to these I'd add that adjuncts are less likely to benefit from seeing the same students from one class to the next and one semester to the next. This fact, plus their typically greater course loads and class sizes, means that adjuncts are particularly well served by efficient, effective techniques for handling student names.

A final, practical point comes back to what I learned the hard way my first semester as a TA: learning and using names pays off in better student impressions of you as a teacher, leading to better student comments and ratings at the end of the semester. Within higher education contexts at least, these ratings are a major determinant of career success. At the time of this writing, there's little systematic research on the link between learning names and student ratings. But given that there is research on how students feel more valued, welcomed, and involved when their names are learned and used correctly, it is not a stretch to predict that faculty who make it a point to learn names will be rated higher.

I want to be clear here: like many in higher education, I've been a vocal critic of student evaluations' overriding influence on the career progression and classroom practices of faculty. I think they're a lazy stand-in for more substantive evaluation of what teachers do. I also know that they undermine the careers of people of color, women, and others whose identities put them at greater risk of bias and exclusion in the academy.

But until such time as these things become obsolete, it is a strategic and self-preserving move to ensure that student evaluations are as positive as they can be. This is particularly true for people of color, women, and others who don't fit the stereotypical picture of a professor.[8] Minoritized and historically excluded identities elicit the most unfair aspects of anonymous student evaluations and make it harder to absorb the professional consequences of a crop of negative student ratings. Getting really good at dealing with student names isn't a solution for these systemic problems, but it's one way for individuals to protect themselves from the worst of their effects, without a massive investment of additional work time.

These are all important goals to keep in mind as we work through the techniques in this book. Here's what to expect as we do. First, I'll offer a concise rundown on what happens in the mind when we learn a name. The purpose of this section isn't to dissect various theories in minute detail or provide a formal literature review. Rather, it is there to serve three practical purposes. First, learning about the process will drive home why you almost certainly struggle with learning names, which in turn will help to dissipate the anxiety and frustration that get in the way of improving. Second, because having a conceptual framework in place helps with acquiring new knowledge, having this background will help you pick up the essential techniques presented later in the book. Third, it will give you the tools to create your own techniques—strategies, mnemonics, and in-class activities that will work in your own unique teaching context and that will leverage your own unique set of strengths.

Next I'll present the core techniques for learning names. These will doubtless include a few pieces of advice you've seen before; name learning is, after all, hard enough and important enough that plenty of experts have weighed in on the topic. However, I've tailored the techniques for the types of settings where you're most likely to use them as a teacher, and I've put them in the context of in-class activities and similar things you're likely to be doing at the beginning of the school term.

We'll then take a look at how the theory and practice plays out in the presence of individual characteristics and background. These include quirks of short-term verbal memory that you might not even realize you have. Neurodivergence makes a difference too; we'll look at the implications for name learning when you have attention deficit hyperactivity disorder, are on the autism spectrum, or (like me) have difficulty recognizing faces. Language background—what your native tongue is, and how it maps onto the names you're learning—also matters, and keeping in mind that it can be an uncomfortable subject, we'll look at tips to help you to learn names from a linguistic or ethnic background that differs from your own. Lastly—and this is a big one—there's the impact of aging. This is an area fraught with anxiety and myths, and so we'll take those on before talking about solutions that can balance out the challenges of learning names in middle age and beyond.

In the final section of the book, we'll talk about how to make the most of your newly enhanced skills, and how to ensure that name learning remains a core part of your teaching practice from here on out, even in the case of challenges such as large classes in which learning every name is not a realistic goal. There will be a short guide to a few technology tools that can help with different facets of name learning. These can't do the work for you, of course, and no doubt there will be changes to the tech-tool landscape as some disappear and brand-new ones are invented (possibly, by the time this book goes to press). But the ones that are aligned to our own learning processes can be a major help, especially if you face any of the special challenges discussed in chapter 3.

This roadmap to the book might help you skip around to tailor the book's advice to your current and pressing needs as a teacher. There's nothing wrong with that. But I hope that no matter what you decide to tackle first, you do eventually circle back to deepening your understanding of how name learning works.

1

HOW REMEMBERING
NAMES WORKS—AND
WHY IT'S SO HARD

In the late 1980s, a group of British psychologists accomplished that rarest of all academic feats: they answered a question, clearly and decisively.[1] Or, about as decisively as things ever get in behavioral science, with results that are still standing even this many decades later.

The questions they answered were these: Why is learning names is so hard? What causes learning names to lag so far behind, compared to learning other kinds of information such as what a person looks like and facts about their life? The researchers did so with an ingenious new study protocol that revealed a phenomenon that came to be known as the *Baker-baker paradox*.

Here is how this weirdly named effect works. First, in the "study" phase, research volunteers are shown photos of different fictional individuals and, for each one, are told a name along with a few details about them, often including occupation and, in one variation, possessions the person owns. Exploiting the fact that many common English surnames are also occupations (Baker, Potter), researchers set things up so that in one run of the study, a photo might be of "John Baker," who is a potter, and in another, it is "John Potter," who is a baker. See the trick here? This lets researchers gauge the likelihood that volunteers would remember that association between a photo and the same exact word either framed as a proper name or as an occupation.

These systematically gathered research findings backed up the common intuition that names aren't picked up as easily as other details we might learn about a person, while at the same time ruling out any chance that this disadvantage happens because of anything superficially different about words that happen to be names.

Simply making a word into a name makes it harder to remember. Why? Like any explanation in the field of psychology, there are different views, but a few key ones seem particularly powerful, recurring across time and across different schools of thought. First is the level of meaning associated with a name. In fact, in controlled studies, the likelihood of correctly associating a name with a person is about the same as associating a nonsense word with them (such as "blick").

This raises the question of why meaning is so helpful when we're remembering something. It likely has to do with how knowledge is organized, or represented, within the mind. Many theorists—myself included—think of these kinds of memories as existing within an immense network. Within the network, individual facts, ideas, and qualities are stored in pieces, units sometimes termed "nodes." Nodes that bear some relationship to each other—two related facts, a characteristic associated with a person, and so on—are connected. When you think of one fact, that activity spreads to other related ones via the connections. So, for example, when I think of my friend Sarah, who lives in the Southwestern United States and is the biggest live music fan I know, activation flows between all of those related nodes—thereby making all that information available to my conscious awareness. In other words, I remember it.

It's that rich, frequently redundant set of connections that makes meaningful information so robust despite all the factors that lead to forgetting. Let's say that one set of connections is weak, or I can't quite get enough activation to a particular node in the network. There are so many interconnections between all the things I know about a person that no single point of failure can block my recall. Just being told someone's occupation, for example, triggers a wealth of potential connections and spin-off facts—what their workplace looks like, what sorts of things they say and do at work, skills they have, what they wear on a typical day, and so on. This network of related facts lights up when the subject of that occupation comes up, creating a robust likelihood of being able to access that qualitative information.

Contrast that to what happens when I'm told a person's name. As more-or-less arbitrary labels, names hang out in isolation, bereft of all those spontaneous associations. There might be a sparse few that come up—the ethnicity or nationality I perceive in the name, whether I think it's unusual or particularly appealing—but nothing like what is touched off by even the most mundane of non-name facts.

This messy, network-style organization of meaningful knowledge is the one reason why struggling with names is so common. But amazingly, there are other reasons as well. Being able to pull someone's name out of memory is a perfect example of a *retrieval* task, in which you have to formulate a response. This contrasts with *recognition* tasks, in which you are responding to information that's provided. Ask your students if they'd rather take an essay test or a multiple-choice one, and they'll tell you—it's inherently more taxing to retrieve than it is to recognize. So while we might commonly equate learning names and faces, it's not a fair comparison at all. Most of the time, when we set about recognizing a face, it is right in front of us. All we usually attempt to do in that situation is judge whether we've seen it before and in what context (the intro class that meets on Tuesdays, the gym, someone we saw on TV).[2]

By contrast, when you're trying to say a name, it demands a more precise response, compared to when you're just deciding whether a face is familiar or is that of a stranger. This last piece of actually verbalizing the information is one final hurdle, with an obscure twist of cognition that turns out to make a big practical difference. When you listen to someone's name, those sounds are represented in your mind in terms of their auditory characteristics. Technically this is called *input phonology*, and, as with judging faces, it's largely a perceptual recognition task. But to say the person's name, we have to tap into a totally different set of representations called *output phonology*—which captures the steps for retrieving and vocally producing those sounds. It's a fine distinction, and it's true that input and output phonology have a lot in common. But they're still different, and thus—especially if you haven't practiced saying a particular name very much—you can fail at that very last stage of coming up with the sounds of a name. It also explains why you might have heard a name before, nodded your head confidently, then drawn a total blank when you tried to say it later.

Let's say you actually did learn the name when you heard it the first time, and that you successfully created the representations for not just how the name sounds but also that all-important output phonology. Are you out of the woods then? No, because there's one last way that name recall can fail even when you've learned it correctly, and it's one that you may be increasingly familiar with as you've gotten older. This is the *tip of the tongue* phenomenon, which is exactly what it sounds like—feeling like the word is right there, but stuck, eluding you in the most maddening way.

Believe it or not, among psycholinguists the tip of the tongue phenomenon (TOT for short) has been the subject of stacks of research articles and more than a few heated theoretical debates. One of these studies is particularly close to my heart and is part of my origin story as a cognitive psychologist. When I was in Introduction to Psychology my first year of college, I was assigned to do what almost all students in my field have to do at some point—volunteer to be a human subject in a faculty research project. I signed up for one that asked me to carry around a little stapled-together paper diary for two weeks, in which I would record any episode in which I was trying to remember a particular word but found that it produced the familiar feeling of being stuck on the tip of my tongue. The data, I later found out, were analyzed and used to develop more precise ways to measure TOTs in the laboratory. They were also compared against results from healthy older adults living in a nearby retirement community, which for the first time demonstrated that TOTs increase as a normal part of aging. When I read the debriefing form explaining the study hypothesis and pondered for myself what has to happen in order for us to complete this everyday cognitive function, I was hooked—going on to work with two of the authors of the study, Deborah Burke and Donald MacKay—as a graduate student and research collaborator.[3]

This study and many others elevated TOTs to the status of being an important and revealing phenomenon. This is because these errors neatly isolate several otherwise difficult-to-pinpoint processes that go on during language production, and also because mapping out how and why TOTs happen is a great way to test out whether a theory of language and memory really does align with the ways human beings speak and remember. We won't get too deep into those theories here, but suffice it to say that TOTs arise at the stage of output phonology, where one weak link between a particular word and its component sounds can sink the whole process. This leaves your verbal system in limbo, having completed the first step of accessing the representation for the word but being unable to finish the job.

This explanation jibes nicely with the subjective experience of being absolutely sure of the specific word you want (as opposed to waffling among various possible synonyms, unsure of which one is right). It also explains why TOTs seem to afflict mainly rare words that you haven't used in a while, as the connections involved in the output phonology weaken with disuse. Lastly, the theory explains another quirk that has been backed up by laboratory studies: the fact that hints can instantly cure a TOT, but only if they are a particular sort of hint. Let's say, for example, that you are trying to say the name "Buckminster Fuller" when your TOT hits. Someone can feed you all kinds of meaningful tidbits about the legendary architect, futurist, and inventor, but it won't help, because TOTs don't happen at the level of meaning. Only sound-related cues (such as that molecular structures known as "buckyballs" are named after him) will do the trick by restoring the missing links in output phonology.

TOTs can happen to any infrequently used word in your vocabulary. But proper names are notorious for giving rise to these frustrating errors of recall. And thus, it's not enough just to have a weak level of familiarity with a name. You need strong connections, well-established representations in memory, and strategies for when the retrieval process breaks down anyway. And as the research has by now established, TOTs commonly increase with age. If you've noticed this issue yourself, don't panic—TOTs for names and other infrequently used words are *not* a sign of impending dementia or brain disease. But they're one reason why we'll take up the issue of aging in more depth in chapter 3.

Most of the time, TOTs are one relatively minor problem among all the other issues with remembering names. More often, we haven't learned the names correctly in the first place or haven't reinforced the output phonology enough along the way. But taken together, all of these issues with creating then retrieving our knowledge of names should robustly demonstrate one of the main takeaways from this book: having trouble with names is the rule and not the exception.

I emphasize this not just to make you, the reader, feel better about whatever failures led you to pick up this book in the first place. It's also necessary groundwork I want to lay for all the techniques and strategies and advice to come. In learning names, forewarned is forearmed, and that initial stage of vigilance—where you don't expect names to come easily—is what you'll need if you want both to learn about effective techniques and to develop the habit of putting them into practice.

Now that we've looked at all the ways that learning names can go wrong, let's flip it around and consider what goes on when we manage to get them right. To do this, let's set a foundation with a brief review on some key concepts from memory theory—ideas that I think all teachers should know at least a little bit about,[4] and that are going to be helpful as we work through the techniques and advice in the rest of this book.

Memory theory has gotten a bit complicated since the original days when researchers thought of memory like an assembly line, one where information comes in through eyes and ears, sits in short-term memory for a few seconds or minutes, then gets automatically shipped off to long-term memory.[5] But we in the field still do lean on several concepts that make it a lot easier to think about and talk about the processes involved.

The first of these concepts is the idea of *encoding*, which refers to whatever happens to create a lasting impression of information in memory, something that turns a sensation or idea into the "code" of thought. Nobody knows exactly what encoding entails, but on the microlevel of the brain, it's likely that it involves the creation of new interconnections between neurons, or reinstatement of a pattern of activity among already-connected neurons. In practical terms, encoding corresponds to learning something new—in other words, putting something into your stored knowledge that wasn't there before. For this reason, encoding is the most important of these memory processes to the topic of name learning; if encoding doesn't happen at the outset, none of the other processes much matter.

The next key process is *storage*. This one is definitely less exciting, because it is just what it sounds like—leaving the newly encoded information alone until you need it again. Like physical items left in storage, memories can fall apart with disuse and the passage of time. They can also be overwritten by newer memories of a similar type, as when the new crop of this semester's students supplants and starts to wipe out the memories of last semester's students.

Finally, there is *retrieval*, the process of reactivating or otherwise pulling back up memories that you've stored. Retrieval turns out to be surprisingly important and not at all simple, especially in the case of names. Unlike, say, a computer's search function or well-organized paper filing system, your brain retrieves a bit differently depending on context and the cues it starts out with, making it less predictable and definitely more prone to drawing a blank. Exactly how the process happens is another thing for the theorists to argue about, but I favor an explanation that harks back to the network idea described earlier in the chapter. Essentially, retrieval involves having activation spread from a cue to stored memory representations via connections. These cues can be meaningful concepts (Buckminster Fuller came up with the idea of domes as living spaces), or they might involve a situation or context (Buckminster Fuller was mentioned in the first chapter of that book I was reading on the plane). Either way, your success at correctly recalling the thing you set out to is going to depend on your starting point and how strong those connections are.

This raises the question of how connections get stronger in the first place, and as it turns out, one major way is through the process of retrieval itself. Recalling something (especially if it's done spontaneously on your own, without cues or external aids) strengthens the chances that you'll be able to retrieve it again in the future. This phenomenon is called *retrieval practice*, and it has turned out to be a gold mine of memory and learning advice—which we'll also lean heavily on in the next chapter when we talk about effective name memorization strategies.[6] Essentially, retrieval practice creates a virtuous cycle by which the more you remember something, the easier it is to do so again, possibly because frequently used connections get better at carrying more activation (i.e., stronger).

Now, a word about where all of these different processes are happening—meaning, within the various subsystems of memory. Memory may not work like a conveyor belt, with information moving mechanically between work stations, but most theorists today do believe that there are at least two distinct forms of memory. These include one form that's immediate or short-term, and one form that's dormant or long-term.

Working memory, or WM as it's often abbreviated, holds a small amount of information in a highly active state, usually so that we can do something with it in the immediate here and now. Oftentimes that information includes some combination of memories that we've pulled up from long-term memory. While we're actively working with this information, in a sense, it exists in two places—long-term and working memory.

Consider what happens when you're trying to log into some account or website on your phone and you receive one of those six-digit security codes. You look at the number and then probably vocalize it to yourself, repeating it as you toggle over to the site where you need to type it in. This process involves retrieving the representations for the numbers from long term-memory, setting them up in the correct order in working memory, then keeping them active by some strategy such as silently rehearsing or visualizing them. It works, but only if you stay focused and if the amount of information is limited to what you can repeat in the space of a few seconds.

That attention connection turns out to be especially important because working memory and attention are incredibly interdependent (so much so that some theorists think they are the same exact thing). Get distracted or start thinking about something else, and the contents of working memory are overwritten in an instant. That fact, in turn, is important because the process of adding new items to long-term memory frequently starts with constructing those knowledge structures in working memory.

I say "frequently," and not "always," because the current thinking among memory theorists is that you don't *have* to repeat and rehearse in order to learn; in fact, most of the important experiences you remember in your life didn't sit around in short-term memory but were instantly incorporated into long-term memory. New words, however, do have to make that kind of a stop in order to end up in long-term storage, and researchers have figured out where they do.

New words do so in a subarea of working memory specialized for holding verbal information. It's known as *phonological working memory,* or PWM. This component lives somewhere between working memory and your verbal comprehension systems, and its sole purpose and function is holding onto sequences of word sounds. It's related to, but distinct from, the output phonology system that I mentioned before, the difference being that PWM holds a record of how words sound (input phonology), not how to say or articulate the sounds.

PWM is what your mind relies on in scenarios like the security-code task, a situation that forces you to hang onto a set of fairly meaningless words (numbers in this example) in a specific sequence. That artificial task isn't PWM's main reason for being, of course. Its real purpose is new word learning, a process that forces you to turn a previously meaningless sequence of sounds into a new, long-term memory representation.[7] PWM kicks in when you hear a brand-new word, buying time for you to set up new representations in your mental lexicon for that new word, including what it means, and in the case of a name, who it stands for.

It's a specialized job, but a critical one, and it's complicated by the fact that PWM capacity varies a fair amount from person to person. I'm going to avoid getting too bogged down in the debate over precisely how much can fit in PWM, but we can ballpark it at around four[8] to eight distinct items. This estimate is also a bit fuzzy because the word length matters. Given that PWM does work a lot like a tape loop, you can hold fewer long words like "refrigerator," compared to short ones like "bed."

Four to eight items is a pretty big spread, and the variability is enough to create noticeable differences in performance, especially in the case of long words or names (which, it is safe to say, take up more of your limited PWM capacity). Researchers have discovered a wealth of interesting connections to real-world vocabulary development. PWM size predicts how well individuals do over the long term at verbal learning tasks, including how large their vocabulary grows to be in childhood, as well as the likelihood that they'll become fluently multilingual.[9] We'll return to this issue in chapter 3, when we talk about factors that might make name learning harder or easier, and how to compensate if your PWM happens to be on the lower end of the spectrum.

Let's now consider how all of these systems work together to successfully get a new name into your long-term memory. First, you have to be attentive, which allows you to notice that there's a new name that you want to remember. You break down the sounds of the name using your systems for analyzing input phonology and then load those phonological pieces up into PWM. There, these word sound representations will stay fresh for a limited time, while you actively work on forming a new representation in long-term memory. This process involves connecting up the sound of the name to related aspects of what you know about that person, such as a visual representation of their face, the context that you know them from (school, the neighborhood, and so on), and any other meaningful facts. These connections all have to link back to the unique representation for that one person. You can think of this as a central hub with spokes leading both to the meaningful facts about the person and to the all-important output phonology that captures how to say that person's name.

Let's come back, full circle, to where we started in this chapter: why names are so hard to learn. It should be evident by now that this process involves quite a few potential points of failure. The encoding stage can fall through (if, for example, we're distracted or never noticed the new name to begin with). Storage can be another weak link, given that the record of the name decays as long as it's not being actively used. Technically, it's debatable whether there really is a decay function that applies to items stored in long-term memory, or alternatively, if interference—the "overwriting" phenomenon—is more responsible for forgetting. For our practical purposes, though, the end result is similar—if you don't use it, you lose it. And even if you haven't actually lost that name in memory forever, temporary retrieval failures result in the frustrating experience of having a name on the tip of your tongue.

In short, there are a ton of ways in which your memory systems can and probably will drop the ball. It's not a fun fact, but realizing it leads to the last factor that can help us get better: *metacognition.*

Developing knowledge and skill about your own learning capabilities—what you're doing right now as you read this book—is central to the concept of metacognition. The last decade or so in education research has seen a boom in interest in metacognition, with one study after another[10] concluding that it isn't just *what* you know, but your understanding about the process of acquiring knowledge in the first place, that makes the difference between struggle and success when it comes to learning.

Metacognition involves a few distinct facets, several of which are particularly relevant to learning names.[11] One is having knowledge about how memory and learning work in general. This is especially helpful when coupled with a type of growth mindset focused on the fact that minds and brains are fully capable of changing with experience—in our case, having the belief that we aren't stuck with having a "bad memory for names" forever. Another facet is having a repertoire of proven strategies that work for different kinds of material. There is also the ability to accurately predict your own performance so that, for example, you know if you've studied enough or if you still need to work on something you're trying to learn.

That last part about accurate prediction can go off the rails, even in highly successful learners. Usually with metacognition, the story is a straightforward one of overconfidence, with most people rating themselves as above average at tasks involving memory and attention.[12] With names, though, the picture is a strangely mixed one. On the one hand, especially as they get older, people are less likely to rate themselves as better-than-average at remembering names in general.[13] But when they're actually in the process of learning names, people are likely to overestimate the likelihood that they have successfully memorized any given one.

In one study of this phenomenon, research volunteers were asked to do something a lot like the original Baker-baker task, learning both names and non-name facts about fictional individuals. The difference was that the volunteers also made *judgments of learning*, or JOLs, as they went along. This addition to the standard procedure let researchers track how confident volunteers felt about the facts they were memorizing. Average JOLs were about the same for names and other facts presented to the volunteers, even though—in line with previous studies—actual performance was much worse for names. In other words, the volunteers did exactly what so many of us do when meeting a new person: they assumed they would pick up the name easily, despite how unlikely that is to actually happen.

The good news is that when the volunteers had the chance to compare their JOLs against their actual scores, their JOLs got more accurate over time, and the volunteers also began allocating their study efforts in more strategic ways.[14] In sum, the tendency to have poor metacognition about name learning is real, but it's easily modifiable with a bit of feedback and reflection.

As education professionals, our metacognition for academic learning is probably good. Metacognition for name learning, by contrast, tends to start out at a much lower level. In this way, strengthening name-learning abilities might offer one additional side benefit—the opportunity to put ourselves back in the shoes of learners who are just starting out, much like our students are, in trying to learn how to learn.

Name learning is a great way to get to know your own memory and what it is capable of doing when the right strategies are in place. Before we get much further into those strategies, there are a few additional distinctions I want to draw, to make what comes as clear and useful as possible.

First is the difference between actually memorizing a name and using it in communication. There are, after all, situations where you might be able to use names perfectly well without memorizing them first—leaning on aids such as those handy plastic name tags on lanyards given out at conferences. In classes, this might take the form of table tents, pieces of heavy paper folded in half and set up on the desk that are a popular approach for those teaching large classes, and one we'll revisit in chapters 2 and 4. In this book, I will presume that most of the time "using" means "remembering" and will focus on that latter process. But in order for the work of memorizing to be worthwhile, you do have to also remember to use the names in conversation. This can be surprisingly difficult to remember to do (especially if you're used to *not* recalling names easily), so I hope that reading this book helps you establish the habit of using names.

The next distinction is a much more consequential one: the issue of learning and using pronouns that match gender identity. Psycholinguistically speaking, pronouns are a completely different issue than proper names, and thus you'll see that in this book, the main focus is on the latter. Practically speaking, though, they are highly related, and both play a major role in creating a respectful, personalized, and inclusive class atmosphere.

Here's a short summary of why pronouns work differently than proper names (and thus need to be treated separately in advice to teachers). Pronouns are much less dependent on the memory processes I described earlier in this chapter. Rather, they tap into the algorithms your language processing systems use to ensure that different components within a sentence agree with each other (for example, in number or verb tense). You don't need to encode and retrieve pronouns separately for each person you're talking to, but rather, must choose the right one based on the number and gender that fit the meaning of the sentence.

As with proper names, you do have to notice and correctly encode a person's gender identity when you first meet them[15] for this process to work properly, but this is less a matter of stringing together word sound sequences in working memory, and more a matter of creating the right conceptual, or "semantic" representations for that person. Once those aspects are in place—meaning that you have firmly established in your memory that that person is, for example, nonbinary, male, or female—your language systems should naturally assign the correct pronoun when you're speaking.

Or to put it another way: proper names are all about individuating a person, and pronouns are about associating them with the right group.[16] Names hinge on creating one unique identifier for a person, while pronouns hinge on connecting that person to characteristics shared by others with that same gender identity. Toward the end of the next chapter, we'll talk about practical strategies that flow out of these principles of how pronouns work. But for now, know that there are reasons why I've chosen to treat names and pronouns separately in this book, and that if you learn how to handle both, you and your students will reap the benefits.

2

THE KEY TECHNIQUES

There's a basic sequence of steps in strategic name learning that I wish I could summarize with a really clever acronym. Alas, the stars didn't line up to make this the case, but even so, at least it's pronounceable: ASAR, which stands for *Attend, Say, Associate, Retrieve*.

Any name-learning system is going to feature some subset of these steps. But I believe that they're most powerful when they are all combined because all the steps are necessary if we're going to make the most of the name-learning processes described in the previous chapter. Together, they make up a set of habits that will take time and effort to establish, but will give as close to a guarantee of strong performance as we're ever going to get.

Attend

Learning by osmosis is a myth, and any new learning requires attention, period. Noticing and focusing when we're introduced to someone is a simple but essential habit to build.

Say

Output phonology is the weakest link in name recall. Strengthen it by using the new name at least twice right away. Ideally, do this out loud, perhaps by using the name a few times in the conversation with your new acquaintance. As a bonus, this will lead you back to step one if you've neglected to pay enough attention by immediately flagging the fact that you didn't pick it up initially. It will also alert you to correcting any mispronunciations, an important thing to do *before* names get too engrained in your memory. Don't be shy about asking "did I say that right?" and inviting the person to correct you.

Associate

While that all-important output phonology is fresh in mind, start building up other connections relevant to the person you're trying to remember. If they're a student, what class are they in? What do you notice about your surroundings, the way the conversation is going, how you're feeling emotionally? Are there facts you can start incorporating into memory—where they are from, what they like to do when they're not in school? None of these connections can save you after the fact if steps one and two have already fallen through, but taken together these personal facts can create a richer set of associations that can help lead you back to who this person is the next time you need to use their name.

The best kind of associations, if you can come up with them on the fly, are cues that tie something easy to remember about the person with specific aspects of their name. This is similar to the *keyword technique*, a mnemonic (memory trick) that's useful for vocabulary memorization, such as what you're faced with when learning a new language. The keyword technique has been described by many authors; essentially, it means coming up with an image that links two words together.[1] For example, a student trying to memorize the fact that, in Spanish, *rodilla* means "knee" might come up with a mental picture of a cowboy riding off to the rodeo on a skinny horse with his knees sticking out on either side. Because mental imagery tends to be a lot more memorable than sounds,[2] that image will stay with you, its key features connecting two otherwise-unrelated words.

A Word on Name Mnemonics

Could you use the keyword technique for names, making up some kind of memorable link that ties to an image and cues the sounds in the name—say, a rhyme or association connected to something about the person's appearance? Sure, but there are a couple of major limitations to keep in mind. First, crafting really effective mnemonics can take more time than you have. Unless you can stall for at least ten to thirty seconds (an eternity in a typical social exchange), you might run out of time. Furthermore, the cognitive load associated with frantically trying to put one together might divert you from the all-important task of making sure you heard and retained the sounds of the name in the first place.

Worst of all is the possibility that whatever you come up with could be embarrassing or insulting, if for some reason it were revealed to the listener. It's altogether too easy to make associations based on a social or physical stereotype; you can probably come up with a few examples on your own, so I won't belabor this further. Suffice it to say that if your mnemonic is something you'd be mortified to explain to the person's face, steer clear.

Some more benign ways to create mnemonics include associating the new person with someone you already know, if you're fortunate enough to discover such a connection. For example, I have an uncle named Hal, a reasonably distinctive name that you don't see every day. If I meet a new Hal, I can quickly notice anything that might remind me of my uncle and use that as the key connection between the two. It's hard to mess up an innocuous link such as this one; even if I were to mistakenly call the new person by my uncle's middle name (Edwin) it wouldn't be the end of the world. That is, like with any other mnemonic, you can accidentally activate an incorrect connection (like a middle name or synonym for a word) when using this familiar-association strategy, but those are unlikely to be as problematic or embarrassing as other kinds of associations to a person's name. Linking to celebrity names (as long as they're generally liked and noncontroversial) can work too; if the Emma you met reminds you of Emma Stone, or your new colleague Beau conveniently resembles Beau Bridges, it's fine to take advantage of that fact.

Mnemonics are complicated, potentially socially awkward, and rarely efficient. The good news about them, though, is that they work well as initial supports, fading away seamlessly as the new knowledge solidifies. They're a good tool to have in the toolkit, just not one you want to rely on too heavily.

Retrieve

To ensure that your hard-won newly learned name actually lasts, you have to practice using it, ideally by pulling it out of memory. Letting the new name go dormant for some period of time, then trying to recall it, is an example of retrieval practice, the superstar memory technique mentioned in the previous chapter. Piles of empirical research[3] all point to one big truth about memorization: actively retrieving a memory is the best way to strengthen it.

Retrieval practice gets dicey, though, when you are working with material that's so difficult that you can't dredge it up well enough to practice even a little bit. In other words, retrieval practice only works when you have a reasonable chance of successfully recalling the information. This is where a variation on a strategy known as *expanding retrieval practice* can save the day. Expanding retrieval practice has you start with a small core of one or two items to remember, rehearsing just those at first in closely spaced time intervals. Then you gradually lengthen the amount of time between rehearsals. You can do this by adding in new items a few at a time, cycling back to the earlier ones as you expand the set. Think of it like one of those folk songs where new verses build on the first ones—such as the "Twelve Days of Christmas" carol in which each round brings in a new gift and also recaps the earlier ones, with more and more time elapsing between rehearsals of each individual gift.

In a simple one-to-one introduction, it's easy enough to see how the ASAR sequence would play out. You'd pay attention when you hear the person's name then you'd repeat it, perhaps using a stock phrase like "Nice to meet you, __." You'd do this "Say" step promptly, before the name has exited working memory, and you'd ask to hear it again if needed. Next up would be some fast thinking as you focus on encoding any qualitative information about the person, the context where you're meeting them, and maybe a quick mnemonic that could bridge the sound of the name with a visual cue. Lastly, you'd circle back to the name after it's faded from your working memory. You might drop it into the flow of conversation, or use it in another "It was great talking to you, ___" type of stock phrase as you're wrapping up the encounter. Bonus points if you rehearse it a few more times later on, such as on the car ride home or the walk back to your office.

With these techniques, learning a few new names at a party is, if not easy, fairly straightforward. Dealing with a whole classroom's worth of names on the first day of the semester, however, is on a whole new level. The next part of this chapter focuses on that new-class scenario, a situation that can overwhelm even the most skilled name learner. It's geared to group sizes of up to about thirty-five, which I personally find is my limit for how many new names I can learn at one go. Don't take thirty-five as a fixed parameter of human memory, however. There's no theoretical basis for setting an upper limit for this type of learning; for example, in memorization competitions, people can learn fifty, one hundred, or more new arbitrary associations at a time, provided that they have the right strategies and are well-practiced at using them. Your limits might be different, so feel free to explore them—the only caveat being that doing pair introductions in groups of over thirty-five people will also eat up too much time to work well as an icebreaker.

The First-Day "Introduce Each Other" Icebreaker

Here's an approach I've used successfully semester after semester in my classes, and also in professional workshops I've facilitated. (After all, students are not the only people who get more out of an experience when the leader knows their names.)

The activity is essentially one big session of expanding retrieval practice for you, the facilitator. It is also structured to offer opportunities to do all the steps in the ASAR process. The twist is that your audience doesn't know you're doing any of this, because they're engrossed in a fairly engaging introduction activity while you're doing your attending, saying, associating, and retrieving. The activity also doubles as a way of eliciting meaningful tidbits of information you can start incorporating into your mental representation of each new person you're meeting. Last of all, it's simply a friendly way for everyone to get to know each other.

First, tell the class (or workshop group, etc.) that you're going to go around the room and have people introduce one another. But, the process will be different than what they're used to doing. Instead of introducing *themselves*, people will pair up and introduce their conversation partners.[4] So for example, when my turn comes, instead of saying, "Hi, I'm Michelle Miller, I work at Northern Arizona University, and I like to knit for fun," I'd say something like, "Hi, this is Rick McDonald, he works at Coconino Community College, and he really likes to ski."

In order to do that, participants will have to get some basic information about their partners. To facilitate this, set a timer for a brief period, about eight to ten minutes, when partners will talk to each other in a brief, informal mini-interview. Each pair should take turns asking each other a few questions, with the goal of ensuring that participants can say a few words about their partner, including, of course, their name.

In setting up this unfamiliar exercise for the group, I start by framing it as an alternative to the traditional introduce-yourself ritual, in which you go around and say your name and something about yourself. I share with the group that I'm convinced that students don't learn a thing from this, given that they spend the first part of the time obsessively rehearsing their own introductions, then the rest of the time rehashing how they must have sounded, hearing basically not one word from anyone else. (This usually draws a few knowing chuckles from the group.)

Getting back to what happens once you've set up the activity, be sure to monitor the time closely, as I have found that it goes by astonishingly quickly once the conversation gets under way. You'll probably want to give a signal at the halfway mark to make sure that all students have had a turn to talk about themselves. Then you'll go around the room, giving each pair about one minute for each person to say a few words about their partner.

Let's now turn to what you, the facilitator or instructor, will be doing to learn names during this exercise. Once you get the initial conversation rolling, you don't have to do much, but it's a good time to walk around and eavesdrop a bit, seeing if you can catch names here and there and begin rehearsing those as a head start.

That is what you will be doing until the time for the initial discussion is up. At that point, you'll reconvene the group and give the signal for them to start going around from person to person as people introduce their conversation partners (again, trying to keep it to about a minute per pair).

As this pair introduction process is going on, your ASAR process will kick into high gear. Here is the sequence of steps to take while the introductions are happening:

Mentally divide the pairs into groups of four to six. (This is easy if the space is already organized into tables or rows, but you'll have to draw mental boundaries around groups if it's not.)

As you listen to each introduction, say something like, "Hi, __," or "Welcome to the class, __." (If you didn't catch the name, ask the speaker to repeat it for you.)

Make some associations, such as a mnemonic or other cue, with the name of the person who is being introduced. (If you can't come up with an appropriate mnemonic quickly, you can skip this step.)

After you've said the name and made associations for the person who's currently being introduced, go back and silently rehearse the names you have heard already. This is the expanding retrieval practice piece of the activity. Start with the first person who was introduced and work your way back up to the present one. This can be as simple as glancing back at that person and silently saying their name to yourself.

When a group of four to six (a table, row, or other set that you've mentally grouped together) has all finished their introductions, thank the participants and then say all the names of that small group out loud again, using a phrase like, "Thanks for those introductions, __, __, __, and __ ."

As you get farther around the room, you might not have time between introductions to rehearse all of the names starting at the very beginning. At this point, you can start your expanding retrieval practice somewhere midway through the group. You can also glance around and choose a few to rehearse at random, or alternatively, concentrate on the ones who seem hardest to remember.

Once you get to the end of the introductions, if you feel confident that you've picked up all the names, you can attempt the big reveal: state that you're going to try to remember everyone. Starting with the first person who was introduced, go around and try to say every name. It's okay if you stumble on a few—group members can correct you if that happens, and if you get most of the names, your group is still likely going to be surprised and impressed.

Wrap up with a transition into the next activity or item on the group agenda. In my research methods class, for example, I challenge the class to come up with hypotheses about how I pulled off the name-learning feat, and this leads into discussion of how those hypotheses might be empirically tested using the types of methods we'll be learning about in the methods class. In my psycholinguistics class, we discuss the Baker-baker paradox and why learning names is so complicated, as a preview of material to come later in the course. Especially if you're doing this at the outset of a course, if you can find a direct link between the ice-breaker and class concepts, definitely use it. This type of active learning is especially valuable on the first day of class, when expectations are being shaped and you're looking to stoke curiosity about the material.[5] Or, if you can't find such a direct link, it's fine to just pivot to the rest of the day's material.

Through using the full ASAR toolkit, learning twenty to thirty names at a go is doable, but it's still challenging. I'd advise borrowing a technique from stage magicians, and don't promise the name memorization feat in advance. Spring it on the audience as a surprise, and only if you feel reasonably confident. If all you do is conclude the exercise by thanking everyone, no one will be the wiser, because as a group icebreaker it still works well. Just be sure you have a backup plan for the transition to the rest of the class or meeting.

In many years of using it, I've found that this activity is a great way to kick off a course, even without the name angle. In terms of first impressions, the buzz of friendly conversation is also a refreshing alternative to the traditional but deadly dull overview of the syllabus that we often do during the first part of the first class meeting.

Furthermore, this activity is one of the more introvert-friendly icebreakers you can do. Having a short-term goal (i.e., being able to say a few words about your partner) makes small talk more structured and easier to approach than typical conversation. The one-on-one conversation format is also less overwhelming than trying to interact with a bigger group all at once. I let students know that if they're nervous about doing the introduction in front of the class at the end, it's fine to take notes as a support. It's a lot less socially awkward to read off of a prepared sheet when you are talking about someone you just met a few minutes ago, as compared to reading a prepared statement about yourself.

Another wonderful side effect of this icebreaker—whether or not you can pull off the whole thing as a feat of memory—is that students are almost guaranteed to leave that day having gotten to know at least one classmate. That one social connection, having a classmate who knows your name and vice versa, can form a nucleus of belonging that helps students forge positive connections throughout the rest of the semester.

One last note on this activity: don't panic if people in your group already know each other, because the structured pair interview still tends to work well. In fact, one of the liveliest icebreakers I've ever hosted was with a group of coworkers from a publishing company I was visiting as a workshop facilitator. Some of them had worked side by side for years; I was the only bona fide new face in the room. But once the discussion got under way, I could tell that the group was loving the opportunity to learn new things about each other. This has played out for me time and again in other events where people show up with their buddies, coworkers, and familiar colleagues. Just ask your audience to play along, and you'll probably see the same thing happen.

Variations, Additional Strategies, and Bordering-on-Cheating Shortcuts

Practicing First with Pictures

When I ask my students how they think I managed to memorize their names on the first day, someone always says, "You did it ahead of time with our school ID photos!" And, they are usually right, at least to a degree. Today's faculty, after all, don't have to bring a Polaroid to class to create a study deck of class photos (something that one of my colleagues used to do back in the day). Most of us can access those photos in advance, either through our learning management systems or the central faculty portal for the campus. I take liberal advantage of this fact, downloading the class list in advance and studying for at least thirty minutes per course before the first meeting.

Does this mean that I can dispense with the in-class activity? Not really. While my students seem to see it as an easy way out, I find that pre-studying photos doesn't reliably ensure learning on its own. It gives me a head start, but I complement it with substantial in-person rehearsal. For one, students often don't look much like their (frequently outdated) official photos. You'll also find that quite a few go by a different name than what is listed on the roster. And, as with any challenging memory exercise, reinforcing what you've learned over spaced study intervals—as you're doing if you study photos then later study faces in the actual class environment—is a powerful mechanism for getting the learning to last.

All those caveats notwithstanding, pre-study is much better than winging it. If you do get to do this, be sure to use effective techniques. Don't just superficially skim the photos—engage in retrieval practice, attempting to actually remember the names like you would with flashcards. Expanding retrieval practice also works well here—start with the first person, retrieve the name, then add a second, go back to the first, retrieve that person and keep repeating that process. As you make your way through the whole group, try randomly picking a few here and there, so you don't get too dependent on the way in which they're ordered.

Ask Students about the Meaning of Their Names

In this variation on the introduction icebreaker, you go around the room and ask students to tell you something about the meaning of their names—the origin, original meaning, or why their family chose it for them. In my case, I'd get to introduce myself by first and last name as "She Who Is Like God, Grinder of Grain"—with my first name also reflecting how my Baby Boomer parents were caught up in a name craze touched off by the Beatles' late-sixties megahit "Michelle" from the

Rubber Soul album, resulting in my sharing a name with millions of other Generation X girls the same age.

How fun is that? It certainly can be, and I've seen it work myself in a seminar or two led by my thesis advisor, Donald MacKay, back in grad school. He was no stranger to the Baker-baker paradox and knew that the elusive linkage between the sound of a name and what it means is key to the name-learning problem. This version of the name icebreaker goes directly to that issue and can trigger some indelible associations in a short space of time.

It can also be spectacularly awkward, or worse. You wouldn't want to do this one-on-one with someone you just met. And like what many teachers now realize about those old-school "family tree" type assignments we did as kids, name histories are fraught for some people. If you've got a small group of students who are on the older or more mature side, it could work, especially if it's practical for you to frame it ahead of time with the reasons why it works (say, in a cognitive psychology course) or to discuss explicitly the different feelings and concerns that might come up in the discussion (as in a social work, teacher education, or counseling course).

Cheating with Cards

Another surreptitious way to work on your name learning for the class is to couple it with some kind of *class-room assessment technique*, or CAT, meaning a short activity done during class time that results in some tangible product, outcome, or assignment. The definitive guide to these is the book *Classroom Assessment Techniques: A Handbook for College Teachers*, by Thomas Angelo and Patricia Cross.[6] However, you can also find lots of examples and condensed explanations of CATs online.[7]

Classically, CATs aren't graded, but I like to offer a few points for these in-class activities, which taken together make up a "class participation" component of students' overall course grade. My favorite is something similar to Angelo and Cross's "minute paper," which has students briefly write down their thoughts on a prompt I give them, usually something asking them to react to or summarize concepts they've just encountered. I do this using one of the most versatile instructional technologies ever invented: the index card. As students are finishing up their cards and filing out, I can check them in one by one, saying, "Thanks, Caleb!" "Have a great day, Dejah!" and so on. If that's too slow, you can rehearse by picking a few at random each day. The main thing is to incorporate some kind of tangible short activity into most or all of your class meetings (which is a really good thing to do anyway, as a form of active learning), and make your own name review part of it.

Table Tents and Name Tags

In classes where I don't do the introduce-each-other icebreaker on the first day, this is my fallback: having students write their names in big letters on folded pieces of card stock, which then sit displayed on their desks. They bring the tents to class each day, at least for the first few weeks. Never one to miss an opportunity for an arts and crafts project, I also bring an array of markers and stickers so that those so inclined can add flair to their tents. Name tags would work too, although you can't beat the tent for reusability and visibility, even from across the room in a big lecture hall.

And it is in these large, anonymous-feeling classes where tents have been shown to have an outsize influence on student perceptions, especially the perception that the professor knows their names. In the study "What's in a Name? The Importance of Students Perceiving that an Instructor Knows Their Names in a High-Enrollment Biology Classroom," name tents were a key feature of the large science course that researchers Katelyn Cooper, Brian Haney, Anna Krieg, and Sara Brownell focused on. Students created card-stock tents and used them every day of the semester, a practice that clearly made an impression on them. When questioned on an end-of-semester survey about whether the professor knew their names and, if so, how the professor learned their names, most said that it was through the tents. Whether or not students were correct in this assumption, this finding demonstrates that tents help create the impression that names are important and that the professor is putting effort into learning them.

There turns out to be another good outcome of the table-tent practice: it helps students learn and use one another's names. By making it easy and socially expected to address one another by name, these little aids help create the classroom atmosphere of collegiality that we all want. This is one reason why Kelly Hogan and Viji Sathy, authors of *Inclusive Teaching:*

Strategies for Promoting Equity in the College Classroom,[8] recommend tents as a key strategy for advancing inclusion. Building on this idea, I think that tents can level the playing field, so that more than only the most vocal and most extroverted students or those who have the easiest-to-remember names are included.

There's not much of a downside to name tents, and they certainly take the pressure off in those first few weeks. But you still need to retrieve, actively practice, and use student names if you're going to remember them over the long haul. Mere exposure over time doesn't create learning (if you don't believe me, I could quiz you on all the various flyers you've walked by in your department's breakroom for the last six months, and it's a safe bet that you would have no clue what they say).

You could even combine the icebreaker with table tents. In this approach students would create their tents on the first day, before they do the pair introductions, enabling you to get an early start on your expanding retrieval practice while they're talking. If, after the partner introductions, you want to attempt to go around the room naming everyone, just have them lay their tents face down first.

Techniques for Correctly Using Pronouns

Recall from the previous chapter that pronouns involve different processes than proper names, but are equally important for creating inclusive, welcoming interactions with students. It makes sense, therefore, to have some techniques at the ready to ensure that you'll consistently use the correct ones.

As with proper names, pronouns start with the initial stages of attending and encoding. You need a beginning-of-term routine and set of habits where you pick up that one crucial fact as soon as possible, in the early stages of building a mental representation of that new person. If you don't already have a space or process where students are invited to provide preferred pronouns[9]—consider setting one up.

In some contexts and institutional cultures, it might not be workable to ask all students to affirmatively state the pronouns they use. If it is workable to ask, though, I highly recommend that you do so. Including a clear invitation to provide pronouns can result in a wealth of benefits to your students, over and above the practicalities of ensuring that you learn the pronouns correctly from the outset. In one study of healthcare communications among adolescents, for example, asking for and making good-faith attempts to use the correct pronouns was far and away the number one factor cited by LGBTQ+ youth as something that created a supportive environment for them.[10] And of course, providing your own pronouns is another way to smooth the way for students to give you theirs.

Ideally, you'll get a new acquaintance's pronouns during the encoding stage, when you are first building new knowledge about them. But regardless of how or whether that happens, try to stop and consciously acknowledge that you're forming a concept of gender when you first encounter the person.

Once you do have a correct concept of a new acquaintance's gender identity, that concept needs to become strongly tied to the mental representation that you are forming of that person. For that to happen, you'll need to begin forming meaningful associations involving their gender—for example, male, female, or nonbinary. This might be hard at first, given that we might naturally be a little uncomfortable thinking about, for example, what gives a person femaleness or what it means to be nonbinary. It's natural and okay to feel uncomfortable; you don't have to share with anyone else what these gendered qualities are in your mind, or even articulate them to yourself in excruciating detail. But you will have to elaborate on those gender-based associations in some way to get pronouns right, because having a meaningful understanding of a person's gender is what will trigger the correct pronoun to surface in the split-second and cognitively demanding process of speech production.

That ultra-fast pace is one reason why we make speech errors all the time, and misgendering mistakes are no exception. Just as we need to give ourselves grace for forgetting proper names, we also need to be able to take pronoun mistakes in stride. That said, there are some special considerations here. Even more than getting a name wrong, misgendering is a potentially hurtful experience for the person we're speaking to. Especially when it happens repeatedly or despite corrections, it becomes a form of microaggression.[11]

If and when you commit a misgendering mistake, correct yourself, acknowledge the mistake, apologize, and move on—actions that the LGBTQ+ youth in the aforementioned study said they highly appreciated.

Do realize, however, that while misgendering is something you may be able to recover from, interpersonally speaking, it's a red flag that something is off about your mental concept of that person. Stop, reflect, and concentrate on repairing it so that it aligns with that person's correct gender identification.

In this chapter, I've shared with you what I consider to be the essential toolkit of evidence-based techniques for learning names and for using correct pronouns. All of these strategies put the typical teacher in an excellent position to learn and use names in a typical class setting. But not all situations are typical. In the next chapter we'll consider variations that make it harder— both in the situation and in the mind of the person who's doing the learning.

3

COMPLICATIONS, CHALLENGES, AND SPECIAL CIRCUMSTANCES

The strategies laid out in the previous chapter provide a solid foundation for name learning in most situations. However, there are some ways to fine-tune and modify them for different individual factors and settings. In this chapter, we will review these additional considerations. I've broken them down into several broad groupings. First, there are the characteristics of you, the person learning the names, with special focus first on neurodivergence. This set of characteristics falls under what psychologists would term "individual differences"—factors that set people apart, even though they tap into underlying processes that people generally do have in common.

Next, we will look at a special case of cognitive difference, the normal aging process. Given that, especially in higher education, the teaching workforce tends to skew older, this is one that will affect most of us at some point in our careers—if it isn't doing so already.

After discussing how aging figures in, we'll look at another factor that can, in theory, affect anyone:

learning names that originate in a language that you're not familiar with. It's something that, as I note in that section in more depth, can be uncomfortable to talk about given that it goes directly to issues of ethnic and racial identity, as well as equity. Techniques drawn from cognitive psychology and psycholinguistics can be helpful for understanding and overcoming the challenges of learning names outside your native language background; while this doesn't make the challenge or the associated discomfort disappear, it can help us direct productive effort in the right direction.

Individual Differences

Limited Phonological Working Memory (PWM)

In chapter 1, I described a component of working memory whose only job is to hold onto word sounds. To recap, PWM gets involved when you have to retain a set of items that can't be turned into a meaningful over-all interpretation, such as when you're trying to type in a security code or hang onto a phone number long enough to write it down. Functionally, PWM's real purpose is to support learning new words. When an unfamiliar sequence of speech sounds comes in, it saves them in a buffer that works a lot like an old-school loop of audiotape, replaying them in a process that subjectively feels like saying the words to yourself, silently.

In the case of names, PWM functions to hold onto the way a name sounds. In the meantime, mechanisms involved in long-term memory create new connections that link the sound of the name to the memory of that person and to associated information such as where you know them from (class, work, the neighborhood, and so on). If you're engaged in the ASAR process described in the previous chapter, you'll also be repeating the sounds out loud, thus reinforcing the output phonology that goes along with all the other newly created memory representations for your new acquaintance.

Generally, the PWM does this job well, enabling us to acquire new names, and add to our vocabulary in general, throughout our lifetimes. However, PWM is also one of those mental capabilities that varies a fair amount across individuals. While PWM capacity usually falls within a range of about five to nine words' worth of information, some individuals are below that typical range. This isn't cause for alarm, nor is it a sign of an underlying disease or disorder. But it does create complications for name learning.

To illustrate, consider a case study published in the early nineties by Alan Baddeley, the pioneering researcher who created our modern-day theory of working memory.[1] The study presents the case of a graduate student in his early twenties, dubbed "S. R.," who happened to show the classic pattern of memory performance associated with extremely low PWM.

Most telling was a pair of tests that tapped the ability to hang onto sequences of words that are devoid of meaning, or nearly so. One is *digit span*, in which you say back random sequences of numbers, and the other is *nonword repetition*, in which you say back word-like nonsense terms like "laib" or "sheal."[2] You can get a handle on whether a person's PWM is particularly low by comparing these results to those from other working memory tests where the to-be-remembered items have some meaning, such as lists of actual words. Most people do worse on nonwords compared to words, because memories for real words can be held in other buffers besides PWM, mental components that are specialized to hold onto meaning and even visual imagery. The disparity in performance between the two—words minus nonwords—is a direct reflection of how much PWM contributes to that person's working memory performance.

In the case of S. R., this normal disparity was wildly accentuated, so that he could only say back a tiny number of nonwords, despite more typical performance on words. Critically, this pattern didn't reflect a general issue with memory across the board, as the young man scored well on other general memory tests (and, as the researchers noted, was performing just fine in a challenging academic program). But when the researchers tried to teach him new words that had to be learned by sound–in this case, new words in Finnish, which was foreign to him—his performance plummeted. He also had reported extreme difficulty in passing required foreign language courses, so much so that he'd received an exemption due to a learning disability. Researchers didn't ask S. R. to try to remember new proper names, but it isn't hard to make the leap between learning new, foreign words and learning names.

This unusual pattern of performance reflected a truly selective, word-specific deficit, one that S. R. might never have known about had he not fallen in with a friend group of cognitive psychologists in grad school. It's not clear why the deficit happened, either. PWM deficits can happen as a result of injuries to the left side of the cerebral cortex, and in fact, it was these more extreme and sudden examples of impaired PWM that led psychologists to develop their approach for pinpointing PWM capabilities. Whether S. R. had experienced a mild brain injury early in life, or whether he was simply on the bottom end of the natural spectrum of capabilities remains a mystery. But his case drives home the fact that PWM capacities vary, and some otherwise typically performing individuals can be at rock bottom in this one arena and never even know it.

Now that I have you thoroughly worried about your PWM, here's how to find out if yours is on the low end of the spectrum.

First the disclaimers: Please don't take any of what I will say about assessing individual differences as medical advice; I see it as advancing your own self-knowledge, not anything like a formal diagnosis. If you sense that your memory abilities or patterns have radically changed, or if those changes seem to be connected to a medical event such as a stroke, please bring that up with a physician right away. However, if you don't have any of these special considerations, feel free to proceed with this informal self-assessment.

DIGIT SPAN

This is the classic test of your PWM power, and it's simple to try on your own. Essentially, it's how many numbers you can reliably hold onto for just a few seconds, long enough to say (or type out) the sequence.

There are quite a few free versions of the test online, but the one offered on the free PsyToolkit site[3] is my favorite. The program administers random number sequences for you to remember and scores the accuracy as you go along. It starts with just one number then works up to longer sequences, until you start getting them wrong. You receive an overall score at the end, which equals the maximum sequence length that you can consistently recall. A span between about five and nine is typical (mine is six). If you are in the five or below range, that is one sign of a relatively low-capacity PWM.

One factor that can have a small but consistent effect on your PWM is the language you speak. When digit span is tested by presenting numbers visually, as it is in the PsyToolkit example I shared, you read the numbers to yourself. Usually, people do this in their native or first language. In languages where spoken words for numbers are very short, such as Mandarin, digit span is longer, contrasting to the pattern seen for languages with long number words, such as Welsh. English number words are on the shorter end of this spectrum.[4]

PHONE NUMBERS AND OTHER RANDOM CODES

Code numbers are an in-the-wild version of the classic digit span test, so if you perceive that you have a particularly hard time hanging onto the latest Google security code long enough to type it into the login window, that is another clue about your PWM. The same is true if you have a hard time writing down phone numbers you've just heard. Do note that we aren't talking about retaining these sequences over a longer period of time; remembering your old phone number from when you were a kid or your hotel room number after you've gone out for dinner tap into different memory mechanisms that don't have much to do with PWM.

LEARNING WORDS IN A FOREIGN LANGUAGE

One final clue is how hard you've found the task of acquiring vocabulary when learning a new-to-you language. As people who've successfully earned at least one degree, most teachers have attempted to become conversant in more than one language, and some have lived abroad for extended periods of time. Thus, we teachers can often think back on our own experiences with building a brand-new lexicon in a new language and get a sense of how easy or difficult this was for us personally.

One caveat is that foreign language learning involves a whole lot more than just acquiring vocabulary; many important components such as grammar, idioms, and the finer points of pronunciation don't have much to do with the PWM. But foreign-language vocabulary definitely taps PWM, to the point where translation equivalents in an unfamiliar language are frequently used as experimental stimuli in academic studies of people with PWM deficits.[5]

Your own capability for learning foreign language vocabulary isn't something I suggest you try to quantify with a high degree of precision, and in real-world learning situations, it's perfectly possible to devise strategies to get around PWM. If you're determined to learn those new words, you'll find a way, which can mask any limitations you might have. However, being a seasoned student yourself, you probably have a good subjective sense of whether this particular type of learning comes easily to you or not. If you've historically struggled in this department, you can count yourself as PWM-challenged.

As I've tried to stress here, low PWM is neither an emergency nor a sign of anything that's gone wrong in your brain. But compensating for it needs to be a part of your plan to build name-learning skill. One of the main ways you can do this is simply to allow extra time in the Say and Associate phases of learning. As with a lot of cognitive processes, speed-accuracy tradeoffs happen, so that more time pays off in better performance. This approach will work best if you also take time to break down longer names, in particular. Because PWM works a lot like a literal tape loop, it gets overwhelmed and fails when it hits its time-limited capacity, which for you might be just a few syllables in. Unfortunately, there isn't an exercise or technique that will expand your overall PWM capacity. But awareness and extra time can help.

Attention Deficit Hyperactivity Disorder (ADHD)

This form of neurodivergence has recently elicited a lot of discussion both within education circles and in the culture at large. Much of the conversation has focused on ways to support students with ADHD, but what about instructors who themselves share this characteristic?

This is a particularly personal question for me, as an individual with ADHD. My ADHD was not discovered when I was a student myself—not surprising given that I am female (a risk factor for under-diagnosis) and, being a Gen Xer, grew up in a time of nearly nonexistent accommodation of or interest in neurodivergence of any kind. I therefore have personally borne the brunt of many ADHD-unfriendly practices in my own educational history. The advice I'll share will reflect my own personal experience as well as what the research says.

In this short book, I won't try to offer a comprehensive definition of what ADHD is, address the various controversies or common misconceptions about the disorder, or encourage you to self-diagnose or self-treat ADHD. But given the disorder's prevalence, and the far-reaching impact it has on a wide range of cognitive processes, it makes sense to include a few practical points for those with suspected or confirmed ADHD.

Although attention is the defining feature of this disorder, memory is also very much involved. This connection reflects the close relationship between attention and memory.[6] Maintaining anything in working memory, in particular, draws heavily on the same neural and cognitive mechanisms that allow us to pay attention. Furthermore, as noted earlier, committing new information to long-term memory almost always requires focused attention.[7]

It follows that performance on memory-intensive tasks would suffer noticeably with even a small decrease in attention. In people with ADHD, this is exactly what happens, creating characteristic patterns of forgetting and memory failure. One psychological measure of these everyday problems, bluntly titled the "Cognitive Failures Questionnaire," prominently features name learning. It asks, first, how frequently you fail to pay attention to people's names upon hearing them and then how frequently you forget those names later on.[8] Even in childhood, kids with ADHD are rated by their parents as being less adept at remembering names.[9]

What should people with ADHD do to compensate for these challenges? It helps to know that the issue starts in the first stages of name learning, where focused attention is key. Attention is what triggers the formation of a new memory for the name, and if that name isn't encoded in memory, no strategy in the world can bring it back.

So, no pressure—but if you, as a person with ADHD, don't consciously notice a name in those first critical seconds, you are almost guaranteed not to succeed. I realize what it sounds like to tell someone with an attention deficit to simply pay more attention, so let me elaborate on how exactly to do that. More so than other people, those with ADHD need to get in a well-established habit of repeating a name when they hear it. If this is you, try setting an intention to listen and repeat, right before you're in a situation where introductions are likely to take place. To prepare, keep in mind that those of us with ADHD are also especially likely to be thinking about a slew of other things once that interaction is under way—what you want to say next, stuff that's going on in the background, various worries and plans for the future, and so on. Social anxiety, which many people with ADHD experience, might also be draining off precious attentional resources once introductions have begun.

With all that to consider, it's important to give yourself permission to ask the person to repeat their name, both immediately ("Nice to meet you, I didn't catch your name though?") and later on in a conversation ("Sorry, tell me your name again?"). It won't be as awkward as you think, and it will help you overcome the significant extra hurdles you have to clear in the early stages of name learning.

Autism Spectrum Disorder (ASD)

A real triumph of the inclusion and neurodivergence movement has been to increase awareness of and challenge myths about autism. More and more, people on the spectrum have been speaking up about their experiences, talking about the coping mechanisms they use and how work environments could be better set up to draw out their strengths.

This is all solid progress toward inclusion, and long overdue. With that in mind, let's consider some special challenges and strategies for those with autism spectrum traits. Surprisingly, even though ASD has been the subject of innumerable research efforts going back decades, its impact on memory functioning is still a bit of a mystery.[10] It is possible that people with ASD have some additional challenges with short-term memory in general, although, even if these do exist, they're likely to be fairly subtle. There also seem to be challenges with using the kinds of organizing strategies that neurotypical people benefit from when creating new memories.[11]

One general link does seem to hold up across studies, though, and it is one that holds special relevance for name learning. As one research team put it, those on the spectrum tend to have "diminished memory for emotion- or person-related stimuli,"[12] something that makes sense in context of the reduced sensitivity to social cues that is characteristic of ASD. Attention might factor into this as well; for those who are predisposed to be less attuned to social interactions in general, it makes sense that they'd be likely to skip over those crucial initial stages of picking up on a new name.

It follows that, much as in the case of ADHD, concentrating one's efforts toward the initial encoding stages is likely to produce the biggest payoff. Focusing and repeating the name a certain number of times can be a key part of a name-learning routine, which over time can become a well-established habit. Fortunately, establishing and maintaining such routines is an area of strength for people with ASD.[13]

One last barrier associated with ASD is difficulty recognizing and distinguishing faces. This isn't a universal experience for those on the spectrum, but for many, it's hard to pair faces to the names they worked so hard to remember. This particular issue can also affect people who aren't on the spectrum, so I've separated it out into the next section.

Prosopagnosia (Face Blindness)

Technically, recognizing and distinguishing among faces isn't a part of name learning. In memory, each name you know is associated with an abstract idea of that person and isn't solely tied to the visual representation of their face. That said, faces are far and away the commonest cue for retrieving names, and practically speaking, knowing names doesn't help much if you can't produce them in response to seeing the person in front of you.

I can personally attest to this last point, having experienced myself the awkwardness of treating an acquaintance like a total stranger. As I mentioned earlier in the book, I have a mild form of the disorder known as prosopagnosia, in which human faces are particularly difficult to recognize and remember. Researchers used to focus mostly on the most dramatic cases of prosopagnosia, instances where the disorder set in suddenly after an injury to the brain. More recently though, there's been recognition that some of us are born with a similar problem. People with so-called developmental prosopagnosia have a lot more time early in life to develop coping strategies, compared to those who acquire the disorder suddenly, and similarly, the brain has more opportunity to rearrange itself in ways that can help compensate. We developmental prosopagnosics may not show the dramatic symptoms that fill classic case studies of brain-injured people (things like introducing yourself to your own spouse on the street, or not recognizing your own face in the mirror). But we do still struggle with the kind of instant visual recognition that others take for granted.

So if you don't relate to the everyday truism "I never forget a face," if you always wondered why bandits in old movies think it's necessary to pull bandanas up to their eyes to disguise their faces, or if you've treated a friend like a stranger because you ran into each other in an unexpected place—this might apply to you. You can find out more tip-offs (along with other useful information and support) online.[14] (If your issues with recognizing faces aren't lifelong, but something that started suddenly or seem associated with new cognitive difficulties you're having, that is more concerning and might warrant medical advice.)

Some of these indicators tie directly to the type of coping strategies you, as a person with face blindness, are probably already using. These include relying on voices, gaits, and hairstyle to recognize people. If such techniques are at all typical for you, your face recognition ability is probably below average. There's no problem with continuing to use these methods, and realizing the reasons for them might help you use them even more effectively. Another practical move can be simply to begin warning people (including your students) in advance about your issue with faces. Using class photos to review names in advance will be harder for you, but it's still worth doing, especially if you can consciously pick out memorable features and start to concentrate on them.

We turn now to two final complicating factors, ones that will affect almost everyone sooner or later. They also tend to activate social sensitivities that make them harder to talk about, compared to what's been discussed so far in this chapter. These include the effects of aging, and what happens when a name originates from a language that is unfamiliar to you.

How Age (Middle and Beyond) Affects
Name Learning

As a demographic, professional educators skew toward the older side. You might not be surprised to know that this does us no favors when it comes to name learning. What might be surprising, though, is exactly why this downward trend occurs.

If you find it getting even more difficult to learn names as you get older, you're not alone: names, specifically, become harder to remember with age.[15] This principle applies both to learning brand-new names and to retrieving names that you learned a long time ago. Especially if it's a name you haven't used in a long time (your sixth-grade homeroom teacher, an obscure celebrity, and so on), you may find that you end up with the name stuck "on the tip of your tongue," a frustrating temporary glitch in retrieval mechanisms that happens more frequently with aging.[16]

That's the bad news. But there is some good news.

Contrary to folk beliefs, not all memory functions get worse with age. This goes back to the fact that memory isn't one system but many, with separate parts that handle longer- and shorter-term retention and also that deal with distinct kinds of information within those long- and short-term subsystems. As it turns out, these varied systems change differently as we get older, with some declining much less than others.

One classic study in the field administered a battery of cognitive tests to UC Berkeley college professors aged thirty to seventy-one.[17] Performance on tests that involved fast reaction times and arbitrary new associations showed the greatest age differences, with declines showing up particularly strongly in the oldest participants. By contrast, memory for meaningful combinations of familiar material showed a completely different pattern. When presented with excerpts of academic-style prose (e.g., a discussion of tribal culture in the Mississippian period), even the oldest professors did just as well as the younger ones at remembering the details of what they'd read.

In general, vocabulary also stays the same or improves with age. Back when I was a graduate student running memory tests at the UCLA Aging and Cognition Laboratory, my lab mates and I saw this demonstrated rather dramatically on standardized tests of word knowledge. Older research volunteers would frequently sail through a fiendishly difficult one involving definitions for obscure words ("prelate," "lanuginous") that stumped our younger control groups made up of UCLA undergraduates. Even in the case of words stuck on the tip of the tongue, the issue is a temporary one; the word hasn't vanished from long-term memory, but rather is inaccessible at the moment.

Notably, however, these relatively age-proof capabilities are ones that don't involve time limits or speed. This gets to one of the core truths of learning names (or anything new) at an older age: it takes more time. Slight changes in the time to learn new information are, in fact, at the center of one major theory of what underlies *all* cognitive aging. According to these "generalized slowing" models, system-wide reduction in the speed of processing introduces errors. This is especially true when working memory or new learning is involved, findings that fit with the patterns of what gets worse and what does not with aging.[18]

It follows from all of this that your best bet at compensating for aging is to simply add more time into the equation. Hearing new names should become your cue to slow down, take an additional moment to focus, and give yourself an extra opportunity to practice. In the case of names you know, retrieval and rehearsal can help save you from exasperating tip of the tongue failures. Researcher Deborah Burke once offered highly practical advice on how to do this: when you're headed into a social situation where you're going to be running into people whose names might have faded over time (parties, committee meetings, and so on), *rehearse in advance.* Think of who might be there and—this is key—don't just picture those people; say their names, ideally out loud.

There's one last major caveat I need to share on the subject of aging. All of what I've said here refers to the typical progression of normal aging, *not* to the changes wrought by age-related diseases such as Alzheimer's dementia. Among those who study cognitive aging, this is an incredibly important distinction. Popular culture may conflate normal aging and dementia (which is perhaps another reflection of our social discomfort with and stereotyping of the topic). But researchers do not conflate the two, pointing out that brain diseases cause changes that are quantitatively and qualitatively different than those that accompany normal aging.

Forgetting important information about people you see frequently (not just stumbling on their names momentarily, but true forgetting), difficulty retrieving common words, and similar dramatic symptoms are all warning signs that warrant a conversation with a physician. By contrast, the more subtle challenges described above in this section—things like needing a bit more time to create a new memory, or temporarily being unable to come up with names you don't use often—are no cause for alarm, nor are they signs of a serious underlying problem.

Names Based in an Unfamiliar Language

One last factor that memory researchers have looked at is the language of origin of names. Forming any kind of new association involving words is harder when the words are foreign to the listener. This principle might not be too surprising to those outside the field, but for researchers, recognizing it was an important step toward teasing out the role of phonological representations in word learning. In other words, how much does already having well-established memories of the individual elements of a spoken word, versus having to create those as you are busy setting up the memories of the rest of the word, matter?

It turns out that it matters a lot. Researchers studying word learning have long known that the amount of overlap in how two languages sound makes a big difference in your ability to learn new words.[19] It's simply more cognitive work to handle a name that involves sounds that aren't part of your vocabulary or that combines sounds in unfamiliar ways. If you already tend to struggle with the working memory aspect of name learning, you may find the challenge goes up even more when you're dealing with less-familiar sounds and syllables.

And even if your working memory is solidly above average, it won't be easy. Simply managing your expectations might dissipate some of the discomfort around this issue. Everyone is unfamiliar with most of the world's languages, and you are no different.

As you might guess, there's no one quick fix for this issue, but the research does suggest where to start—at the level of word sounds, which are the building blocks of the rest of the name. Focus even more strongly than you normally would on these elements, sounding them out (ideally aloud, if you can), until you can assemble them into syllables. And before you memorize the pronunciation of the whole name, be sure that you have the pronunciation correct, or as close as correct as you can.

Most people, in my experience, take it in stride if you ask for feedback on how you are pronouncing their names. If it's a name you'll be using a lot in the future, you may want to search online for an audio clip of its pronunciation (resources addressed more in the next chapter). If you can find a connection to a more familiar name or word, that can help serve as a cue as well. For example, when I met my colleague Yahya, he explained that this unfamiliar-to-me Arabic name had common roots with the super-familiar Western name John, which helped prompt me the first few times I went to recall his name. Because the pronunciation involved sounds I didn't know, finding a recording online was also hugely helpful—as was Yahya's feedback the next time we met.

This peer-to-peer interaction worked out okay, but with students, you are likely to be walking a finer line as far as their comfort with such an exchange. Students with names perceived as "unusual" by the dominant culture have probably already had bad experiences with teachers in the past, and the impact of whatever you say will be amplified in the social spotlight of a class meeting. Egregious mispronunciations on your part aren't the only blunders you might make. Even worse are commenting on the perceived difficulty, Anglicizing or outright changing the student's name, or refusing to try altogether.

Striving to avoid these gaffes is well worth the effort. As Norma Angelica Marrun put it in her powerful essay "Culturally Responsive Teaching across PK-20: Honoring the Historical Naming Practices of Students of Color," "An educator who learns to correctly pronounce students' names signals respect and validates students' racial, ethnic, linguistic, religious, and cultural identities. Learning students' names is the first step in becoming a multicultural and culturally responsive educator."[20]

In short, expect that names new to you will be exponentially harder the less similar the originating language is to your own native tongue. Divide it up, identify any parts that are familiar to you, and test out how you are doing. Consider uploading, or asking students to upload, audio recordings of the pronunciation within your learning management system. And monitor yourself closely to avoid adding to the poor experiences that minoritized students, in particular, have already endured.

In this chapter, I've invited you to reflect on a variety of factors that can make learning names more difficult or more complex, depending on the individual. This is an area where self-knowledge can be helpful in revealing what strategies and shortcuts might be particularly helpful. In the next chapter we'll look at how to put newfound name learning skills into practice, and keep deepening that practice over time. These include some technology tools designed to support name pronunciation and memorization, and ideas for special situations such as extra-large classes.

4

KEEPING UP THE GOOD WORK

Making Name Learning a Core
Part of Your Teaching Practice

Now that you've learned about the strategies available,
I hope that you're excited to put them into practice. As
you might imagine, that "practice" factor is key. You
will get better at this aspect of teaching the more you
work at it, and over time, the shortcuts and heuristics
I've described will start to kick in naturally each time
you hear a new name.

That said, it's important to note that because of the
way complex cognitive skills work, you *will* have to keep
practicing. Unfortunately, there is no one structure or
location in the brain that is your "name-learning center." The components that power your ability to pick
up, retain, and retrieve names are spread out across
multiple regions and structures, precluding any simple
strengthening regimen. Nor does your brain function
exactly like a muscle, so that you could simply work on
building up a given area then end up with a reserve
of strength you could tap into at any time and in any
situation. On the contrary, when you work to develop a

cognitive capability, that newfound power doesn't tend to seamlessly transfer over into new situations; it's not like strengthening a pair of powerful biceps that don't care whether you're lifting a free weight or a gallon of milk. You can get more skilled at using good techniques, and you can develop the metacognitive awareness to know when to use them, but this development over time is more a matter of adopting good strategies rather than creating a permanent, name-specific memorization skill.

But don't let that caveat discourage you. Practice will make names come to you much more easily than they do now, and practice is the only way to identify and master the techniques that work best for you. This chapter lists some resources that can help and exercises that will help you gauge your progress and fine-tune your approach. We'll also consider a few variations geared to very large classes, in which memorizing every single name is simply impractical. There are still ways to reap the benefits of some name learning in these situations, according to some intriguing recent research on student perceptions. And then, we will consider other ways to extend and get value from your newfound skills, including how to encourage students to learn and use one another's names in class, and how to normalize asking for and responding to names in student-teacher interactions.

Practicing Skills

Start by designing some low-stakes practice activities for yourself, ones that will give you feedback right away on how well the systems in this book are working for you. Here's one idea: go to your institution's website and pick a department or unit that you are fairly unfamiliar with that has about five to twenty people associated with it. Find the page that has photos of staff, and go through the list using expanding retrieval practice, covering up the names if you need to as you prompt yourself with each photo. See how many passes through it takes before you can name them all. For extra practice, go back after one day and then after a week to see how many you can still remember. The side benefit of this approach is that you'll know more of your own colleagues by name, possibly making you look like a rock star the next time you're at a school function.

Helpful Tools and Resources

Given that name learning is a nearly universal issue, technology companies have stepped up to provide different kinds of tools to help. These roughly break down into two types: pronunciation aids and aids for keeping track of and memorizing names.[1] They can't do the work for you, but at the time of this writing there are a few in particular that you may want to experiment with.

Pronunciation Aids

RACE EQUALITY MATTERS "MY NAME IS"
ONLINE RESOURCE

This free online set of tools[2] offers audio pronunciation of any name you type in. Notably, it also can produce a phonetic spelling of names, which is useful for (among other things) email communications, note-taking, and email signatures. You can use this for your own name, but you can also encourage your students to use it for their communications as well. There are also helpful instructions for how to double-check phonetic spellings generated by the site, and an overview of why name pronunciation is important for equity and inclusion.

NAMECOACH

This company's[3] sole focus is on technological aids for name pronunciation. Namecoach started in the higher education space but has now branched out to provide corporate- and sales-oriented products as well. These include tools that automatically integrate recordings of name pronunciations into email signatures, and also include access to vast, location-sensitive databases of name pronunciations from around the globe. In the case of higher education, these functions can be integrated into learning-management systems, along with students' names and pronouns, essentially creating a single place where a faculty member can quickly reference everything about how to properly address a student.

Namecoach's single-minded focus on this topic makes it a leader in the industry. The company also shares a strong focus on inclusion and equity that makes its values a good match to higher education. However, a drawback is that the company's products are not something that individual faculty could pick up in say, the iOS App Store. Rather, a whole organization, such as a university or department within a university would contract with it to purchase access that faculty could then use. That said, if this is something your institution has already purchased or is considering purchasing, you should consider taking advantage of it.

PRONOUNCENAMES

Similar to the "My Name Is" resource, Pronounce-Names[4] is a free site where you can type in a name and hear how it's pronounced, with a simple and stream-lined interface. It could be useful, for example, as you are going through your rosters before the semester to get a head start on memorizing names. I can also imagine this being useful in online courses, for example, before videoconferencing with students or when recording audio-based assignment feedback for them. While this site is worth bookmarking, it doesn't have the vast selection of names you might see in a paid service like Namecoach. When I've used it, I've found that even fairly common names don't always have a full recording and explanation, although there might be some other helpful basic information (phonetic spell-ing, rhymes-with, origin of the name, and so on). Still, when I'm recording audio feedback in online courses and going over my new rosters, I've got Pronounce-Names open in a tab for easy reference as I go.

NAMEDROP

NameDrop[5] takes on name pronunciation from the other side; its main function is to help others pronounce your name, through recordings that you make. There are extended features you can get with a paid subscription, but at a minimum, you'll be able to add the name pronunciation to your email signature and get a link to your "NameDrop Page" that you can easily share online. This might be a good resource to share with students as part of your syllabus or welcome-to-the-course email.

Memorization Aids

NAME SHARK

Name Shark[6] has a colorful, simple interface for creating groups of people whose names you want to remember. You upload pictures, then use the app's quiz modes to go through them and test yourself.

NAMEORIZE

Compared to Name Shark, Nameorize[7] is more text-oriented and less photo-oriented, encouraging users to add notes about different people they meet (the contexts where you met them, their jobs, friends in common, and so on).

Other Resources

Besides these specialized solutions for tracking and remembering names, there are also general-purpose applications for organizing professional contacts (such as Contacts Journal CRM[8]) that you can use to file away photos, names, and other information for quick memory refreshers. Also keep in mind that you can use a basic flashcard application to do retrieval practice (which is arguably the most important aspect of any practice regimen you might set up). Quizlet[9] is a perpetual favorite in this category, with an easy-to-use interface for creating general types of virtual flashcard decks. Vocaroo[10] is a free easy-to-use site where you can record and create links to short audio clips, which could be yet another way for you or your students to let others know how to pronounce their names.

There are some guiding principles you should keep in mind as you evaluate new tools that might come out in the future. Any name-learning app will draw its power from the key technique of active retrieval and, in the case of groups of new names, from the ability to tackle them incrementally using expanding retrieval practice. Any application that makes it easy and appealing to do that is your best bet.

What to Do When There Are Too Many to Remember

My personal limit for learning names is around thirty-five in a group. Yours may be higher or lower, but especially if you teach in a high-enrollment field like STEM or social sciences, you'll eventually end up with a class size that well exceeds that limit.

Fortunately though, even moderate efforts to use names in class can create an outsize positive impression on students. The study by Katelyn Cooper and colleagues mentioned earlier provides a fairly precise estimate of this impression. In this study, undergraduates in a large biology class were polled about their impressions of whether the professor knew their names, and, if so, how they thought the professor learned them (along with other questions probing the perceived importance of name learning). Name tents were used in the class, which enabled the instructor to learn and use names during the semester. This particular technique may have also inflated (in a good way) students' estimates of whether their names were known. A large majority (78 percent) reported that they thought the professor had learned their names, when in fact, this was true for only about half of the students (as measured by having professors try to name roster photos at the close of the semester).

The researchers credited the name tent technique for this disproportionately positive impression, also noting that when rating previous courses of a similar style and subject, students estimated that their names were known only about 40 percent of the time. Female students gave particularly low estimates of being known in previous courses, a concerning trend in light of classroom equity. It was therefore particularly reassuring that with the name tents in place, these gender disparities in perceptions were eliminated.

To reiterate a theme from much earlier in this book, learning names and using names are two separate processes but work together to create multiple benefits for students. Especially when the size of the class, special issues with remembering names, or any other challenges make memorization difficult, name tents can help you produce most of the beneficial effects of actually learning the names, as long as you follow through with using them to say students' names in class.

It's also important to note that in the study described above, students weren't only asked to *make* a tent on the first day. Instead, there were also explicit directions to bring and use the tents in subsequent meetings. Students in this study noted that the instructors made a sustained effort to pay attention to and use the tents throughout the semester as well. These efforts did pay off, suggesting that even in a large and seemingly anonymous class, it is worth acknowledging the challenge of names, while committing to doing the best you can to learn them.

The results also encouragingly suggest that learning even a few names will create the illusion that you know many more. Set a goal for yourself—roughly 15, 20, or 30 percent of the class—and be mindful of equitably distributing that percentage across different demographics. Monitor yourself to ensure that you are not focusing on one gender, ethnicity, or other distinct group to the exclusion of others, recognizing that most everyone carries biases that can distort attention to names.

There are also different regions within the room to consider, and the first rows aren't a bad place to start. You can then mentally divvy up the rest of the rows, tables, pods or whatever else organizes the space, ideally into subgroups of about five to ten. If you can, circulate before class and during activities like think-pair-share. This classic in-class exercise involves having students first ponder a question individually, then discuss it with one or two neighbors, and finally, share their answers with the whole class. It provides a bit of free time for the instructor to rehearse student names. This is also something that instructors can do during other downtime in class (such as when students are busy taking a quiz) by glancing around and doing some covert retrieval practice. As you start to gain ground by learning more and more names, try to use them as frequently as you can when answering questions and taking comments. If you don't know the name of a student who is asking a question, quickly ask them their name before responding and then use it in your answer. The same thing applies during the sidebars that happen at the beginning and end of big classes—any student who's coming to talk to you one-on-one should leave knowing that you do now know their name.

An excellent example of many of these techniques in action can be found in Harvard political philosopher Michael Sandel's lectures. I've shown clips from these in workshops before as good examples of dynamic, interactive lecturing; one notable feature that makes them so compelling is how Sandel uses student names on the fly as he builds up a class discussion within the large lecture hall. One favorite is this one[11] on the ethics of military recruiting.

Within this particular video, the active back-and-forth discussion between the lecturer and students starts about nine minutes in if you want to skip ahead (although this masterfully crafted lecture is well worth watching from start to finish). I can't think of a better model than Sandel for how to personalize and add interactivity to a large lecture.

Lastly, a technique that you can use in the larger classes is to create your own practice and study materials with the help of students themselves. One way to go about this is to have students file past a whiteboard on which they've written their own names. They stand under the name while you snap a picture, which you can use to review and study. The picture taking might take a couple of class periods to get through, for a larger class, and you'd want to have ways for students to opt out along with good practices for securely storing and deleting photos once they're no longer needed. (It's also a good idea to consult your institution's guidelines for storing sensitive information before trying this technique.) But by setting up their own database of photos to practice with, a committed instructor could accomplish some truly impressive name learning in return for the time invested.[12]

For big classes, the bottom line is this: even imperfect and incomplete knowledge of student names is worth developing. It's a big improvement over the default of near-total anonymity, as long as you're vigilant to ensure that your efforts and attention are equitably distributed. Name learning is also an important step toward making big classes feel smaller and is one of those areas of teaching where fairly small investments of effort can pay big dividends in terms of student appreciation and engagement.

Getting Students to Learn and Use Their Classmates' Names

Once you're well under way with your own name-learning efforts, you can take it to the next level by encouraging and facilitating the same thing among students. The Cooper et al. article mentioned above was encouraging on this front too, with student comments and responses that all suggest that students will follow your lead if you do make a point of using names. Table tents are a tried-and-true method for making this easier for them to do. Small group activities where students work with a variety of peers throughout the semester, and in which they need to use names in some way, should reinforce this as well.

Ingenious additional ideas can be found in the short article "Activities for Helping Students Learn One Another's Name," by Judith Davidson.[13] My favorites include these two: handing out to each student a class roster at the beginning of the semester, with the idea that they would refer to this "dance card" each day as they get to know classmates; setting up small group discussions by choosing a student to draw names out of a stack of cards, calling names out as they go. Even these small touches can help students learn to individuate their classmates, and that in itself can be the foundation for the social relationships that nourish success in college over the long term.

And this brings us right back to the reasons to worry about learning names in the first place—relationships. Positive relationships, ones in which people feel appreciated as the unique individuals that they are, are the foundation that can support better classroom atmospheres, positive interactions between students, and instructor-student rapport. They are also a step toward establishing trust in you as the instructor, something that's also tremendously important to learning, especially when you are asking students to take risks and adopt new perspectives.

Being able to call students by name lets us catalyze energizing in-class discussions like the ones in Michael Sandel's Harvard course—conversations in which the interpersonal interactions flow so smoothly that the exchange of ideas takes center stage. For those of us who aren't natural community builders or small-talk makers, name learning is a nice compensatory skill, one that even the most introverted people can acquire with a moderate amount of practice.

And perhaps, over time, we can model and encourage students to do things that help us remember their names. They can get into the habit of introducing themselves to instructors when they drop by office hours or come up after class with a question. The more we get out into the open the fact that names are challenging (both socially and cognitively), and help is always welcome, the more welcoming, in turn, our educational communities will be.

I hope the advice I've offered here will help you master name learning as a key strategy for inclusive, student-focused teaching. Now that you've reached the end of this short book, I hope you're excited to apply what I've shared. And when you start getting really good at it, give yourself credit—because you're cracking the code on one of the most challenging tasks our minds can perform. This one question of how we learn names has elicited some of the cleverest, most applicable research and theory in cognitive science that I've seen in my career in the field, work that we can all benefit from.

In this book I've tried to ensure that all the advice I've offered is faithful to that science. But like a lot of teaching advice, I think it will work best when you adapt it to your own style, academic discipline, and philosophy. I encourage you to think about how you'll internalize this key skill as part of your own efforts to create vibrant, enjoyable, and inclusive classes. Try out the activities I've described, keep what works, and ditch what doesn't. And when you invent new ways to help address this universal and age-old teaching problem—don't keep it to yourself! Feel free to add your experiences and your own favorite techniques on a Substack post[14] which I've set up as a way of gathering ideas from readers. No matter what, share your ideas with your teaching colleagues and add them to your growing store of treasured teaching techniques.

ACKNOWLEDGMENTS

I've been fortunate to be able to share the ideas in this book with many of my fellow teachers over the course of ten plus years of running workshops and offering advice. One person after another asked how I pulled off the name-learning icebreaker, enough to persuade me to write up and post the rudiments of the procedure. The enthusiasm and inquisitive spirit of these engaged teachers were the most important catalyst for this book.

After a few more years mulling over whether I ought to turn these bare-bones ideas into a book, things happened quickly once I shared the idea with James Lang and Derek Krissoff. Their excitement at that early stage of the game gave me the push I needed to run with the idea. James's expert guidance, as always, made the book orders of magnitude better than it would have been otherwise. Thanks are also due to Andrew Berzanskis, who is the editorial director of the University of Oklahoma Press and an enthusiastic champion of the recently re-envisioned Teaching, Engaging, and Thriving in Higher Ed book series. Andrew also offered insightful feedback on the manuscript itself— the kind that both tells an author exactly how they can improve what's there and motivates them to see the project through.

This may be a short book, but it was written in a concentrated sprint that meant I needed all the help I could get. My fellow-educator spouse, Rick McDonald, helped keep life's demands at bay, even as he handled his own towering set of daily demands as an elementary school teacher. My sister, visual arts professor Cynde Miller Balent, offered nonstop support, many stories from her own classroom to tap into for inspiration, and an unending supply of the best memes the internet can offer. My mom, Darla Ferris Miller, and her trio of smart, funny, creative sisters—my aunts Karen, Kathy, and Sharlene—also made up a wildly enthusiastic cheering section, one I can always count on to help spark the next big idea and summon the energy to make it happen.

Sprinting alongside me many days was my intrepid longtime writing partner Rebecca Campbell. Whether by Zoom, or by wine bar, we have spent many an hour laughing, processing, and planning—hours that pay off handsomely in the writing output we get at the end of it all. My supporter, friend, and coach-in-a-pinch Gary Schoep asked the right questions that led me to conclude that I truly did want to write this book, and helped me set up systems and processes that would keep me on track along the way.

I'm also grateful for the feedback from peer reviewers Viji Sathy and Robert Talbert, who gave this book a close and thoughtful reading. I'm in awe of the work both of them have done in faculty professional development and in writing useful, engaging books for teachers, and so I was especially happy to get their perspective on the early version of this one. Lori Mumpower gave encouraging feedback as well as I was working to improve the manuscript, including great insights on the differences between pronouns and names.

Good books start with good feedback, and also with a supportive environment. Northern Arizona University, my home institution, has once again affirmed the importance of the work I do via its support for this project, and it has provided an inspiring setting where I can always test and refine new ideas for teaching. I'm especially grateful to the NAU Department of Psychological Sciences chair and associate chair, Ann Huffman and Eylin Palamaro-Munsell, for all they do to make sure our department is the kind of place where great work can happen.

Especially given that this book takes me all the way back to topics I studied as an undergraduate psychology major, I have special appreciation for the people who helped me get a start in the field back then. Richard Lewis, my Pomona College academic advisor and neuroscience professor, instilled in me my own personal mental model of the perfect college teacher, an ideal that I carry with me still today. My lab mate and fellow UCLA graduate Lise Abrams has been a stellar example of a teacher-scholar in action, and I've watched with academic-sibling pride as she's made one lasting contribution after another to the field of psycholinguistics. Most of all, I'm grateful to my undergraduate research mentor, Deborah Burke, and my graduate advisor, Donald MacKay. They were the ones who first took the time to convince me, so many years ago, that the seemingly intangible mental machinations that let us speak, think, and remember can in fact be known, and occasionally improved, through the tools and techniques of cognitive science.

The scientific discoveries that underpin this book, along with so much else of the work I do, came about through the effort of dozens of researchers in cognitive psychology and neuroscience. I hope that the brilliance of their original discoveries shines through as I've worked to distill and apply them to our shared mission as educators: enabling our students to expand their minds and achieve their dreams.

NOTES

Introduction

1. For an idea of the type of research we were doing at the time, see Burke, D. M., MacKay, D. G., Worthley, J. S., & Wade, E. (1991). On the tip of the tongue: What causes word finding failures in young and older adults? *Journal of Memory and Language 30*(5), 542–579. https://doi.org/10.1016/0749 -596X(91)90026-G; MacKay, D. G., & Miller, M. D. (1996). Can cognitive aging contribute to fundamental psychological theory? Repetition deafness as a test case. *Aging, Neuropsychology, and Cognition, 3*(3), 169–186; and Miller, M. D., & Johnson, J. S. (2004). Phonological and lexical-semantic short-term memory and their relationship to sentence production in older adults. *Aging, Neuropsychology, and Cognition, 11*(4), 395–415.

2. Cohen, G., & Burke, D. M. (1993). Memory for proper names: A review. *Memory, 1*(4), 249–263. https://doi.org/10 .1080/09658219308258237.

3. For some examples, see Miller, M. D. (2022). *Remembering and forgetting in the age of technology: Teaching, learning, and the science of memory in a wired world.* West Virginia University Press; Miller, M. D. (2014). *Minds online: Teaching effectively with technology.* Harvard University Press; and Miller, M. D. (2011). What college teachers should know

about memory: A perspective from cognitive psychology. *College Teaching, 59*(3), 117–122.

4. Hogan, K. A., & Sathy, V. (2022). *Inclusive teaching: Structures for promoting equity in the college classroom.* West Virginia University Press.

5. Marrun, N. A. (2018). Culturally responsive teaching across PK-20: Honoring the historical naming practices of students of color. *Taboo: The Journal of Culture and Education, 17*(3). https://doi.org/10.31390/taboo.17.3.04; Tanner, K. D. (2013). Structure matters: Twenty-one teaching strategies to promote student engagement and cultivate classroom equity. *CBE Life Sciences Education, 12*(3), 322–331. https://doi.org/10.1187/cbe.13-06-0115.

6. Eaton, R., Hunsaker, S. V., & Moon, B. (2023). *Improving learning and mental health in the college classroom.* West Virginia University Press; Bruff, D. (Host). (2023, May 2). Teaching for mental health with Robert Eaton and Bonnie Moon (No. 12) [Audio podcast episode]. In *Intentional Teaching.* https://intentionalteaching.buzzsprout.com/2069949/12769655-teaching-for-mental-health-with-robert-eaton-and-bonnie-moon.

7. Cooper, K. M., Haney, B., Krieg, A., & Brownell, S. E. (2017). What's in a name? The importance of students perceiving that an instructor knows their names in a high-enrollment biology classroom. *CBE Life Sciences Education, 16*(1), 1–13. https://doi.org/10.1187/cbe.16-08-0265.

8. Neuhaus, J. (2022). *Picture a professor: Interrupting biases about faculty and increasing student learning.* West Virginia University Press.

Chapter 1

1. Cohen, G. (1990). Why is it difficult to put names to faces? *British Journal of Psychology, 81*(3), 287–297.

https://doi.org/10.1111/j.2044-8295.1990.tb02362.x; Cohen, G., & Faulkner, D. (1986). Memory for proper names: Age differences in retrieval. *British Journal of Psychology, 4*(2), 187–197. https://doi.org/10.1111/j.2044-835X.1986.tb01010.x; McWeeny, K. H., Young, A. W., Hay, D. C., & Ellis, A. W. (1987). Putting names to faces. *British Journal of Psychology, 78*(2), 143–149. https://doi.org/10.1111/j.2044-8295.1987.tb02235.x.

2. Burton, A. M., Jenkins, R., & Robertson, D. J. (2019). I recognise your name but I can't remember your face: An advantage for names in recognition memory. *Quarterly Journal of Experimental Psychology, 72*(7), 1847–1854. https://doi.org/10.1177/1747021818813081.

3. Following is that now-classic article, with my own data in it: Burke, D. M., MacKay, D. G., Worthley, J. S., & Wade, E. (1991). On the tip of the tongue: What causes word finding failures in young and older adults? *Journal of Memory and Language, 30*(5), 542–579. https://doi.org/10.1016/0749-596X(91)90026-G.

4. Miller, M. D. (2011). What college teachers should know about memory: A perspective from cognitive psychology. *College teaching, 59*(3), 117–122. https://doi.org/10.1080/87567555.2011.580636

5. For a much more detailed discussion of current thinking in memory theory, and the relationship between memory, teaching, and learning, see my last book: Miller, M. D. (2022). *Remembering and forgetting in the age of technology: Teaching, learning, and the science of memory in a wired world.* West Virginia University Press.

6. Retrieval practice has also touched off an abundance of scholarship, both theoretical and practical. For just two examples of both kinds, see Karpicke, J. D., & Roediger, H. L. (2008). The critical importance of retrieval for learning. *Science, 319*(5865), 966–968. https://doi.org/10.1126

/science.1152408; and Lang, J. M. (2016). *Small teaching: Everyday lessons from the science of learning.* Jossey-Bass.

7. McQueen, J. M., Eisner, F., Burgering, M. A., & Vroomen, J. (2019). Specialized memory systems for learning spoken words. *Journal of Experimental Psychology: Learning Memory and Cognition, 46*(1), 189–199. https://doi.org/10.1037/xlm0000704; Baddeley, A., Gathercole, S., & Papagno, C. (1998). The phonological loop as a language learning device. *Psychological Review, 105*(1), 158–173. http://dx.doi.org/10.1037/0033-295X.105.1.158.

8. Cowan, N. (2010). The magical mystery four: How is working memory capacity limited, and why? *Current Directions in Psychological Science, 19*(1), 51–57. https://doi.org/10.1177/0963721409359277.

9. Baddeley, A., Gathercole, S., & Papagno, C. (1998). The phonological loop as a language learning device. *Psychological Review, 105*(1), 158–173. http://dx.doi.org/10.1037/0033-295X.105.1.158.

10. For a review of just some of this work, see Bjork, R. A., Dunlosky, J., & Kornell, N. (2013). Self-regulated learning: Beliefs, techniques, and illusions. *Annual Review of Psychology, 64,* 417–444. https://doi.org/10.1146/annurev-psych-113011-143823. Saundra Maguire's books of advice to teachers and students also heavily emphasize the importance of metacognition. See, for example, Saundra, M. (2015). *Teach students how to learn: Strategies you can incorporate into any course to improve student metacognition, study skills, and motivation.* Stylus.

11. Tauber, S. K., & Rhodes, M. G. (2010). Metacognitive errors contribute to the difficulty in remembering proper names. *Memory, 18*(5), 522–532. https://doi.org/10.1080/09658211.2010.481818.

12. Hargis, M. B., Whatley, M. C., & Castel, A. D. (2020). Remembering proper names as a potential exception to the

better-than-average effect in younger and older adults. *Psychology and Aging, 35*(4), 497–507. https://doi.org/10.1037/pag0000472; Miller, M. D., Doherty, J. J., Butler, N. M., & Coull, W. G. (2020). Changing counterproductive beliefs about attention, memory, and multitasking: Impacts of a brief, fully online module. *Applied Cognitive Psychology, 34*(3), 710–723. https://doi.org/10.1002/acp.3662.

13. Hargis, M. B., Whatley, M. C., & Castel, A. D. (2020). Remembering proper names as a potential exception to the better-than-average effect in younger and older adults. *Psychology and Aging, 35*(4), 497–507. https://doi.org/10.1037/pag0000472 https://awspntest.apa.org/doiLanding?doi=10.1037%2Fpag0000472.

14. Tauber, S. K., & Rhodes, M. G. (2010). Metacognitive errors contribute to the difficulty in remembering proper names. *Memory, 18*(5), 522–532. https://doi.org/10.1080/09658211.2010.481818.

15. I'm using the singular "they" here, a practice that also has a lot of support from the psycholinguistic research literature. See, for example, MacKay, D. G. (1980). Psychology, prescriptive grammar, and the pronoun problem. *American Psychologist, 35*(5), 444–449. https://doi.org/10.1037/0003-066X.35.5.444; and LaScotte, D. K. (2016). Singular they: An empirical study of generic pronoun use. *American Speech, 91*(1), 62–80. https://doi.org/10.1215/00031283-3509469.

16. This useful heuristic was offered to me by faculty developer Lori Mumpower, to whom I'm quite grateful.

Chapter 2

1. I'm using an example from Margaret Matlin's textbook *Cognition*, which also has an excellent description of this mnemonic. Matlin, M. (2008). *Cognition* (6th ed.). Wiley.

2. I talk more about this fact about visual imagery in one of my other books: Miller, M. D. (2014). *Minds online: Teaching effectively with technology.* Harvard University Press.

3. For a review, see Karpicke, J. D., & Roediger, H. L. (2008). The critical importance of retrieval for learning. *Science, 319*(5865), 966–968. I also talk a lot about retrieval practice in Miller, M. D. (2022). *Remembering and forgetting in the age of technology: Teaching, learning, and the science of memory in a wired world.* West Virginia University Press.

4. I didn't invent the idea of having partners introduce themselves—I learned about this from a graduate student whose name (ironically enough) I do not remember, in one of my seminars about twenty years ago. It took me a few years after that to couple the partner-introduction idea with name learning.

5. For more discussion of the importance of the first class meeting, plus excellent advice on how to put the principles into practice, see James Lang's advice guide for the *Chronicle of Higher Education,* How to teach a good first day of class. https://www.chronicle.com/article/how-to-teach-a -good-first-day-of-class/?cid2=gen_login_refresh&cid=gen _sign_in

6. Cross, K. P., & Angelo, T. A. (1993). *Classroom assessment techniques: A handbook for college teachers* (2nd ed). Jossey-Bass.

7. For one excellent example, see the following document, which originated at Vanderbilt University's Center for Teaching: https://vcsa.ucsd.edu/_files/assessment/resources /50_cats.pdf.

8. Hogan, K., & Sathy, V. (2022). *Inclusive teaching: Strategies for promoting equity in the college classroom.* West Virginia University Press.

9. The term "preferred pronouns" may be a useful one as it's familiar to many people. However, keep in mind

that some sources favor the term "established pronouns," to avoid implying that using a person's correct pronouns is an optional practice. See American Psychological Association. (2019). *A guide for supporting trans and gender diverse students.* https://www.apa.org/apags/governance/subcommittees /supporting-diverse-students.pdf.

10. Brown, C., Frohard-Dourlent, H., Wood, B. A., Saewyc, E., Eisenberg, M. E., & Porta, C. M. (2020). "It makes such a difference": An examination of how LGBTQ youth talk about personal gender pronouns. *Journal of the American Association of Nurse Practitioners, 32*(1), 70–80. https://doi.org/10.1097/JXX.0000000000000217.

11. Whitley, C. T., Nordmarken, S., Kolysh, S., & Goldstein-Kral, J. (2022). I've been misgendered so many times: Comparing the experiences of chronic misgendering among transgender graduate students in the social and natural sciences. *Sociological Inquiry, 92*(3), 1001–1028. https://doi.org/10.1111/soin.12482.

Chapter 3

1. Baddeley, A. (1993). Short-term phonological memory and long-term learning: A single case study. *European Journal of Cognitive Psychology, 5*(2), 129–148. https://doi.org /10.1080/09541449308520112.

2. One good way to create nonwords is to rearrange the sounds of real words, such as "bail" or "leash." This helps factor out any differences that could be due to the particular sounds themselves.

3. https://www.psytoolkit.org/experiment-library/digit span.html.

4. For more on this cross-linguistic effect on working memory, see Mattys, S. L., Baddeley, A., & Trenkic, D. (2017). Is the superior verbal memory span of Mandarin

speakers due to faster rehearsal? *Memory & Cognition, 46(3)*, 361–369. https://doi.org/10.3758/s13421-017-0770-8.

5. See, for example, Freedman, M. L., & Martin, R. C. (2001). Dissociable components of short-term memory and their relation to long-term learning. *Cognitive Neuropsychology, 18(3)*, 193–226. https://doi.org/10.1080/02643290042000080.

6. For a more detailed exploration of this connection, see my previous book, Miller, M. D. (2022). *Remembering and forgetting in the age of technology: Teaching, learning, and the science of memory in a wired world.* West Virginia University Press.

7. MacKay, D. G. (1987). *The organization of perception and action: A theory for language and other cognitive skills.* Springer-Verlag.

8. Broadbent, D. E., Cooper, P. F., FitzGerald, P., & Parkes, K. R. (1982). The Cognitive Failures Questionnaire (CFQ) and its correlates. *British Journal of Clinical Psychology, 21(1)*, 1–16. https://doi.org/10.1111/j.2044-8260.1982.tb01421.x.

9. Skowronek, J. S., Leichtman, M. D., & Pillemer, D. B. (2008). Long-term episodic memory in children with attention-deficit/hyperactivity disorder. *Learning Disabilities Research & Practice, 23(1)*, 25–35. https://doi.org/10.1111/j.1540-5826.2007.00260.x.

10. Nowicka, A., Cygan, H. B., Tacikowski, P., Ostaszewski, P., & Kuś, R. (2016). Name recognition in autism: EEG evidence of altered patterns of brain activity and connectivity. *Molecular Autism, 7(1)*, 1–14. https://doi.org/10.1186/s13229-016-0102-z.

11. Desaunay, P., Briant, A. R., Bowler, D. M., Ring, M., Gérardin, P., Baleyte, J.-M., . . . Guillery-Girard, B. (2020). Memory in autism spectrum disorder: A meta-analysis of experimental studies. *Psychological Bulletin, 146(5)*, 377–410. https://doi.org/10.1037/bul0000225.

12. Boucher, J., Mayes, A., & Bigham, S. (2012). Memory in autistic spectrum disorder. *Psychological Bulletin, 138*(3), 458–496. https://doi.org/10.1037/a0026869.

13. Bordignon, S., Endres, R. G., Trentini, C. M., & Bosa, C. A. (2015). Memory in children and adolescents with autism spectrum disorder: A systematic literature review. *Psychology & Neuroscience, 8*(2), 211–245. https://doi.org/10.1037/h0101059.

14. One good source is www.faceblind.org.

15. Cohen, G., & Burke, D. M. (1993). Memory for proper names: A review. *Memory, 1*(4), 249–263. https://doi.org/10.1080/09658219308258237.

16. Burke, D. M., MacKay, D. G., Worthley, J. S., & Wade, E. (1991). On the tip of the tongue: What causes word finding failures in young and older adults? *Journal of Memory and Language, 30*(5), 542–579. https://doi.org/10.1016/0749-596X(91)90026-G; Bredart, S., & Vanootighem, V. (2021). Middle-aged people's perceptions of name recall failures. *Advances in Cognitive Psychology, 17*(4), 27–32. https://doi.org/10.5709/acp-0344-z.

17. Shimamura, A. P., Berry, J. M., Mangels, J. A., Rusting, C. L., & Jurica, P. J. (1995). Memory and cognitive abilities in university professors: Evidence for successful aging. *Psychological Science, 6*(5), 271–277. https://doi.org/10.1111/j.1467-9280.1995.tb00510.x.

18. MacKay, D. G., & Burke, D. M. (1990). Cognition and aging: A theory of new learning and the use of old connections. *Aging and Cognition: Knowledge Organization and Utilization, 71*, 213–263. https://doi.org/10.1016/S0166-4115(08)60159-4; Salthouse, T. A. (1996). The processing-speed theory of adult age differences in cognition. *Psychological Review, 103*(3), 403–428. https://doi.org/10.1037/0033-295X.103.3.403.

19. Baddeley, A., Gathercole, S., & Papagno, C. (1998). The phonological loop as a language learning device.

Psychological Review, 105(1), 158–173. https://doi.org/10.1037/0033-295X.105.1.158; Ellis, N. C., & Beaton, A. (1993). Psycholinguistic determinants of foreign language vocabulary learning. *Language Learning, 43*(4), 559–617. https://doi.org/10.1111/j.1467-1770.1993.tb00627.x.

20. Marrun, N. A. (2018). Culturally responsive teaching across PK-20: Honoring the historical naming practices of students of color. *Taboo: The Journal of Culture and Education, 17*(3). https://doi.org/10.31390/taboo.17.3.04.

Chapter 4

1. Cooper, K. M., Haney, B., Krieg, A., & Brownell, S. E. (2017). What's in a name? The importance of students perceiving that an instructor knows their names in a high-enrollment biology classroom. *CBE Life Sciences Education, 16*(1), 1–13. https://doi.org/10.1187/cbe.16-08-0265.

2. https://mynameis.raceequalitymatters.com/.

3. https://cloud.name-coach.com/education/.

4. https://pronouncenames.com/.

5. https://namedrop.io/.

6. http://namesharkapp.com/.

7. Nameorize is available in Apple's App Store.

8. https://www.contactsjournal.com/.

9. www.quizlet.com.

10. https://vocaroo.com/.

11. Sandel, M. (2010). "HIRED GUNS" [Episode 05]. In *Justice: What's the right thing to do?* [Video]. YouTube. https://www.youtube.com/watch?v=8yT4RZyIt3s&list=PL30C13C91CFFEFEA6&index=6.

12. I'm grateful to Viji Sathy for suggesting this technique for learning names in large courses.

13. Davidson, J. (2014, January 24). Activities for helping students learn one another's name. *Faculty Focus.* https://www

.facultyfocus.com/articles/teaching-and-learning/activities
-helping-students-learn-one-anothers-name/

14. https://open.substack.com/pub/michellemillerphd
/p/got-a-favorite-technique-for-learning?r=11slp&utm_camp
aign=post&utm_medium=web.

INDEX